Y0-EOZ-451

LOIS ORSWELL, DAVID SMITH, AND FRIENDS

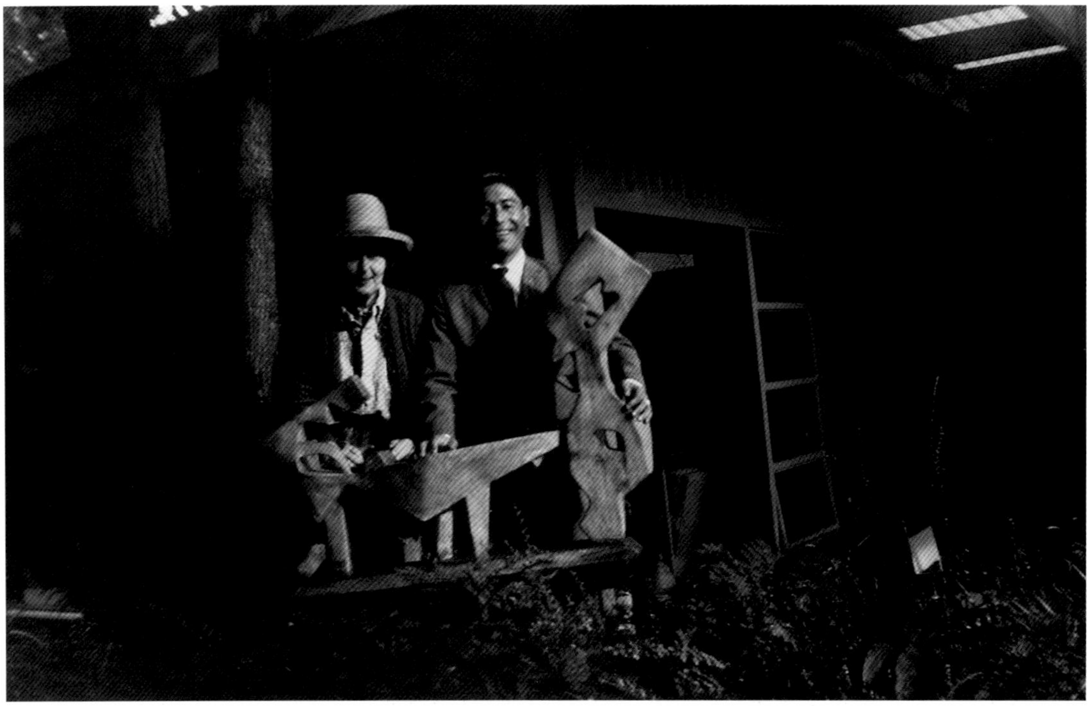

Lois Orswell (1904 – 1998) and Jaime Andrade with David Smith's sculpture *Terpsichore and Euterpe* (1947)*
Photograph by David Herbert at Lois Orswell's home, Bafflin, Pomfret, Connecticut
Estate of David Herbert, collection of Jaime Andrade
*See also Figs. D, E, pp. 11 and 12, and Plate 15, p. 48

Lois Orswell
David Smith
and Friends

WORKS FROM THE LOIS ORSWELL COLLECTION

HARVARD UNIVERSITY

NOVEMBER 14, 2003–JANUARY 24, 2004

This exhibition was organized by
the Harvard University Art Museums
in partnership with Knoedler & Company

Knoedler & Company
– ESTABLISHED 1846 –
19 EAST 70 STREET NEW YORK NEW YORK 10021
TEL 212 794-0550 FAX 212 772-6932 WWW.KNOEDLERGALLERY.COM

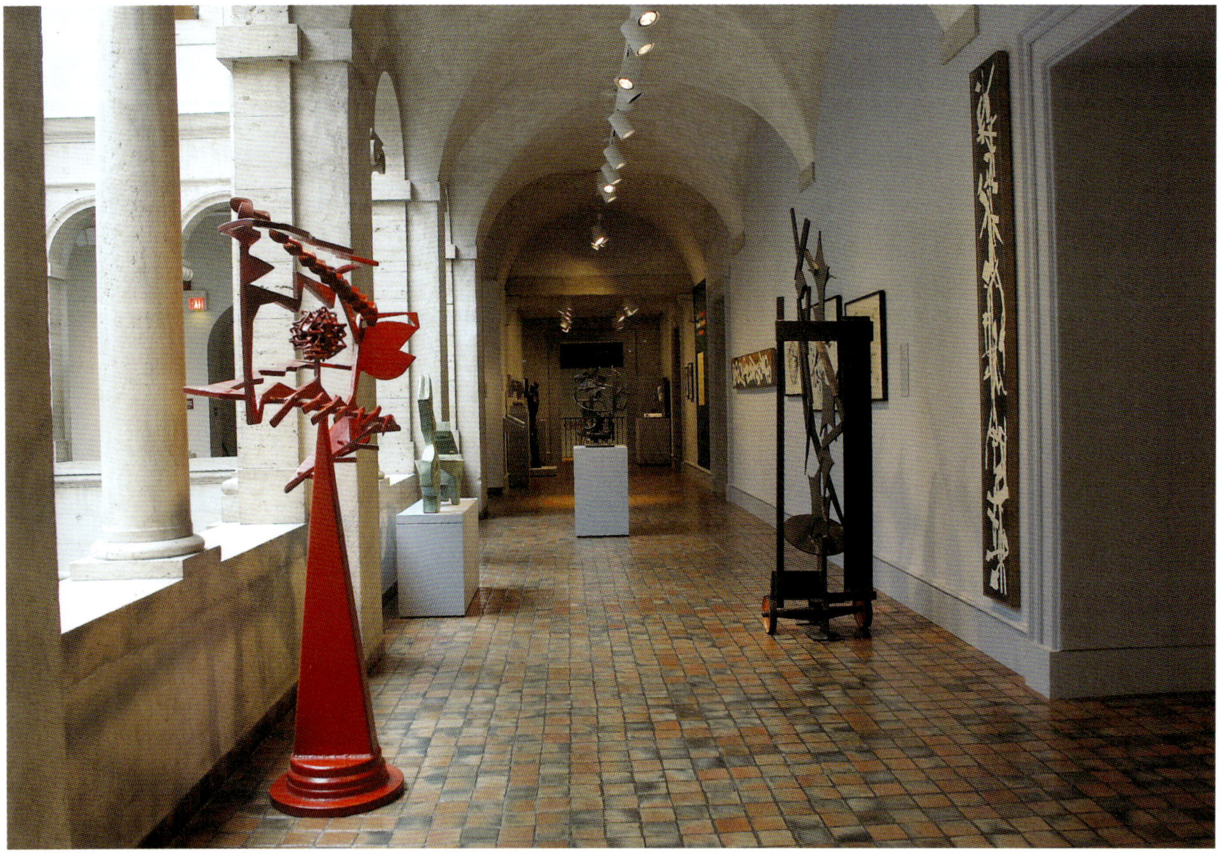

Fig. A. View of the exhibition *Lois Orswell, David Smith, and Modern Art*
Fogg Art Museum, Harvard University, September 21, 2002 – February 16, 2003

PREFACE

L*ois Orswell, David Smith, and Friends* is a celebration of the passion for art that binds us together as colleagues and as friends. Sharing the "vibrations" (as Lois Orswell or "LO" called them) of exceptional works and the excitement of each other's ideas, helped to form the foundation for this friendship. There was one friend in LO's life who has been a dedicated champion of the Harvard University Art Museums, and that is Marjorie (Jerry) Cohn, who has served Harvard as conservator, curator, teacher, and Art Museums acting director.

Jerry's connection with LO's vibrant spirit and tireless love of art played a critical role in LO's decision to leave her collection in the care of Harvard's Fogg Art Museum. LO's gift is part of a remarkable tradition at the Harvard University Art Museums that is fueled by friendship and a mutual dedication to art among directors, curators, scholars, and collectors. Like Grenville L. Winthrop, Edward W. Forbes, Paul Sachs, Maurice Wertheim, Maida and George Abrams, Stuart Cary Welch, and many others, LO's connection to Harvard established an important resource at the Art Museums for teaching, research, and the training of future scholars and leaders in the arts community.

It is with great excitement that we celebrate the first presentation of the Lois Orswell Collection in New York. I want to thank Ann Freedman, the inspired president of Knoedler & Company, for embracing LO, her collection, and the chance to collaborate with the Harvard University Art Museums. We also salute E.A. Carmean, Jr., Frank Del Deo, Per Haubro Jensen, and LO's friend Jaime (Jimmy) Andrade, for their dedication to LO's legacy and for all of their hard work on the exhibition.

Finally, I want to thank Sarah Kianovsky, assistant curator of European paintings, sculpture, and decorative arts, Rebecca Wright, and our conservators and registrars for their important contributions to the project.

Together, this team of friends has created a special opportunity for students, scholars, and curious visitors to explore this "passionate and obstinate" woman and her pioneering collection.

Richard Benefield
Deputy Director, Harvard University Art Museums

. . . *AND FRIENDS*, A FOREWORD

FRIENDSHIP IS THE INTANGIBLE FRAMEWORK of the art world. This exhibition portrays a story of intense friendships, rich in correspondence and mutual support, which describes the bond between the collector, the artist, and the museum. In this compelling story, the collector is Lois Orswell, the artist is David Smith, and the museum is the Fogg Art Museum at Harvard University.

Lois Orswell considered her collection personal and private – an "intimate" family. The works of art became her lifelong "friends." This far-reaching collection, unparalleled in its representation of the work of David Smith, has been donated to the Fogg, and will be forever shared with the public at one of the world's premier institutions of higher education and the visual arts.

The genuine collector is a rare being, a pioneer who assembles a collection on the basis of taste and knowledge. Rarer still is the collector who has the ability to reach into the soul of the living artist, as Lois Orswell did:

> I wanted the COMPLETE artist. . . . For me, David [Smith] became a loyal friend and a most understanding one. . . . He understood my character better than I did and he treated me accordingly. . . . It is good to be trusted, in one's judgment and in one's financial dealings, it happens not very often but I know David did trust me and I appreciated it. I certainly was deeply in earnest about his work and I think that those trips to get it were about the best thing that I ever did . . . I only knew him as a kind and loyal and understanding friend. . . . He was loyal to me and I intended to be equally so to him . . . Now all I own is at the Fogg and I am at peace about it and I do pray he is.[1]

We have chosen the word "friends" in the title of our exhibition, *Lois Orswell, David Smith, and Friends*, to underscore the central role that friendship played in Mrs. Orswell's life as a collector and benefactor, beginning with her view of the artworks themselves as her "close friends." For his part, as an artist, David Smith felt:

> "Most of my work is personal, needs a response in close proximity and the human ratio."[2]

The present exhibition not only reveals the character and quality of Lois Orswell's collection, it also brings to light the unique character and quality of her patronage. Proceeding with quiet determination to discover the defining art of her time, Mrs. Orswell understood the importance of the moment and had the confidence to grasp it. Although her early collecting was briefly featured in *Art News* (1944, 1947) and in *Arts* (1961), she remained largely unknown by the art community at the time of her death, at age 94, in 1998. She decided to live in the remote Connecticut countryside. David Smith, who also desired distance from the New York art scene, chose to live and work in the seclusion of Bolton Landing in upstate New York. His younger daughter Candida wrote: "He eschewed the clamor of New York City's art world. He sought a quiet, far place for the call and response to inner challenges."[3]

Lois Orswell was not concerned with status, social prestige, or public recognition. Her circle of friends was small: a few trusted dealers (including Knoedler at the outset of her collecting), the artists she patronized, and scholars and museum professionals who shared her interests. She acquired steadily and intuitively, not what was fashionable but what she liked. The collection is the result of Mrs. Orswell's fortunate combination of circumstance and perseverance. She intended that her "family" of sculptures, paintings, and drawings would stay together in the museum of her choice – the Fogg Art Museum. This vision was one she shared with David Smith, which notably inspired *his* personal donations to the Fogg.

The legacy of Lois Orswell is one of a long, charitable and cultured life – a surpassing appreciation for the creative process and an unwavering belief in art.

In the fall of 2002, Jaime (Jimmy) Andrade, my friend and longstanding colleague here at Knoedler, came to me carrying a newly published book. "I bought this for you. I knew her," he announced. Opening *Lois Orswell, David Smith, and Modern Art*, I realized this was the catalogue for the exhibition of Smiths at Harvard I had heard about. But I confess, like a great many in the art community, I was unaware of the collector – Lois Orswell.

I began reading the catalogue's compelling biography of Lois Orswell by Marjorie B. Cohn, the curator of the Fogg exhibition, and the revealing correspondence between Mrs. Orswell and David Smith, edited by Sarah B. Kianovsky. I was fascinated, and in February 2003 went to Cambridge to see the exhibition and meet Marjorie (Jerry) and Sarah. The inspiration for this exhibition developed from that first visit. Now, with the generous curatorial collaboration of the Harvard University Art Museums, Knoedler presents an adaptation of the original, marking the debut of Lois Orswell's collection in New York.

Our challenge was to carefully select a focused, cohesive group of sculptures, paintings, and works on paper from the Fogg's extensive

Orswell collection. With the guidance of the Fogg exhibition's curators, Jerry Cohn and Sarah Kianovsky, it was agreed that the Knoedler presentation would reflect Mrs. Orswell's concentration on David Smith – extending from this core group of Smiths to include representation of many of his New York School contemporaries.

The present catalogue serves as a companion to the Harvard University Art Museums' publication of the Fogg's (2002–2003) exhibition. For most exhibitions, the catalogue is prepared *before* the works in the show are gathered together and presented to the public. The Knoedler catalogue then is a sequel to the Fogg's comprehensive study, allowing for responses and further observations, and includes installation photographs of the Fogg's exhibition. In her essay, "Snapshots, Postcards, Telephone Bills: Thoughts on Archives and History," Sarah Kianovsky reflects on the rich experience of studying the Orswell-Smith correspondence and the immediacy and poignancy of the handwritten note. Additionally, three of Lois Orswell's friends have agreed to share their insightful recollections of her – Jerry Cohn, her longtime devoted friend at the Fogg; Hilton Kramer, the distinguished art critic who was, uniquely, a friend of *both* David Smith and Lois Orswell; and Jimmy Andrade, a caring and supportive friend who was frequently a guest in her Connecticut home. This "Orswell Trio" engaged in lively conversations with E.A. Carmean, Jr., a Smith scholar and the curator of the major David Smith retrospective at the National Gallery of Art, Washington, D.C., in 1982. Also included here are previously unpublished personal photographs of Mrs. Orswell at home with her works of art.

The story of this remarkable woman touches us in complex and human ways. Lois Orswell formed her collection as she formed her friendships, with abiding commitment. "No man is the whole of himself. His friends are the rest of him."[4] No doubt, this very personal collection reflects the mind, the spirit, and the eye that created it – and most especially the heart.

Ann Freedman
President, Knoedler & Company

1. Excerpted from a statement by Lois Orswell, "To any one interested," (dated July 28, 1984) reprinted pp. 13–19.
2. David Smith, "Notes on My Work," *Arts Magazine* 34 (February 1960) pp. 44–49.
3. Candida N. Smith in *The Fields of David Smith* (New York: Thames and Hudson, Inc., 1999) p. 17.
4. From *The Good Life Almanac*, quoted in Hulton Getty, *Best Friends: A Photographic Celebration* (New York: William Morrow and Company, Inc., 2000) p. 44.

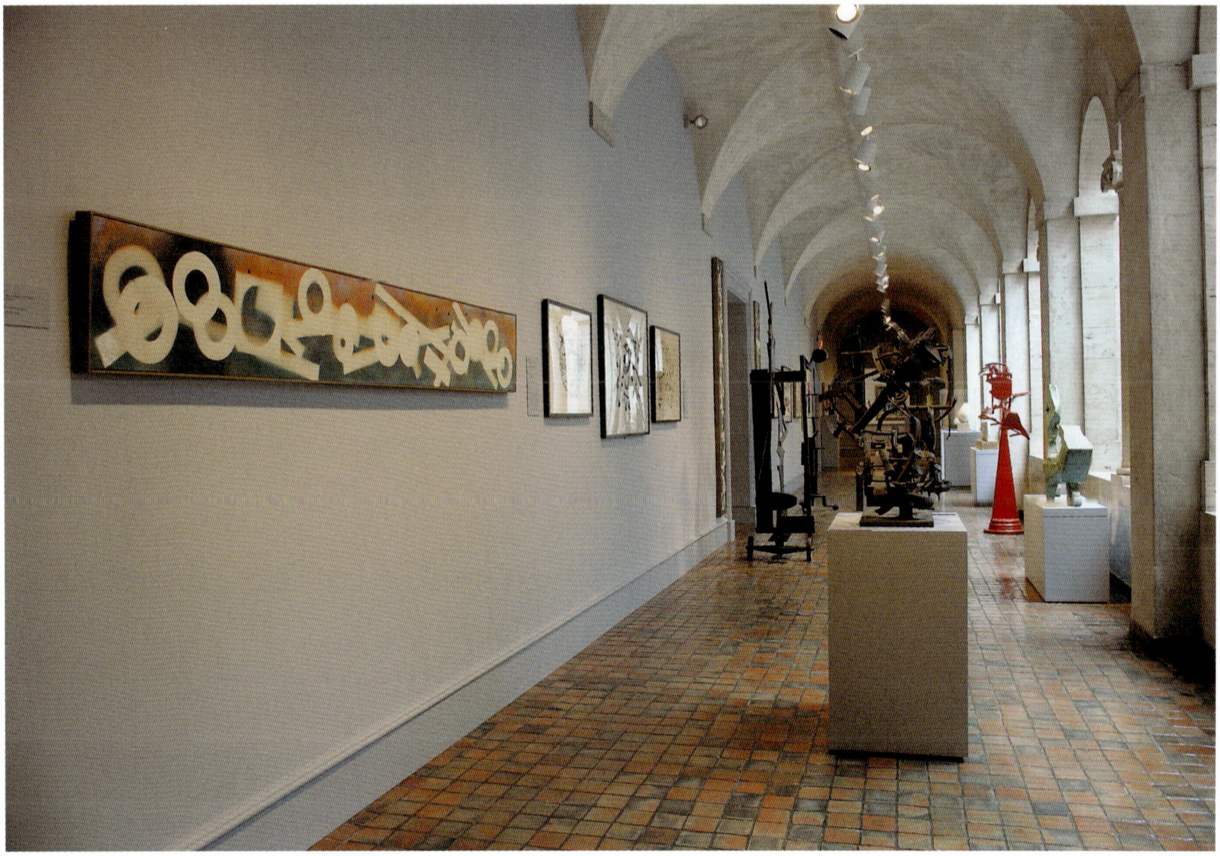

Fig. B. View of the exhibition *Lois Orswell, David Smith, and Modern Art*
Fogg Art Museum, Harvard University, September 21, 2002 – February 16, 2003

SALUTE TO JAIME ANDRADE

LOIS ORSWELL, *DAVID SMITH AND FRIENDS* conveys a message about friendship and the human spirit. In that light and on this occasion, I salute a special Knoedler friend and colleague, Jaime (Jimmy) Andrade. Jimmy has been a presence in the New York art community for over forty years. After more than a quarter century of working with Jimmy at Knoedler, I am more than ever aware of his goodness and grace and the remarkable reach of his friendships.

Lois Orswell was among the many to adore Jimmy. "What a lovely person Jaime is! I wish he were nearer and our lives collided more often," she wrote in the mid-1960s. To honor his friend, Jimmy has made a significant contribution to the present exhibition by sharing delightful stories about his personal friendship with Mrs. Orswell and by lending material from his private collection of photographs and letters. Characteristic of his generosity, Jimmy will donate all of these important materials to the Fogg Art Museum, further adding to the extensive Orswell archive.

Indeed, it is Jimmy's nature to give and to share. His gracious and shining smile can fill a room, and we are all the more fortunate for having Jimmy "nearer" as our cherished friend.

Ann Freedman
President, Knoedler & Company

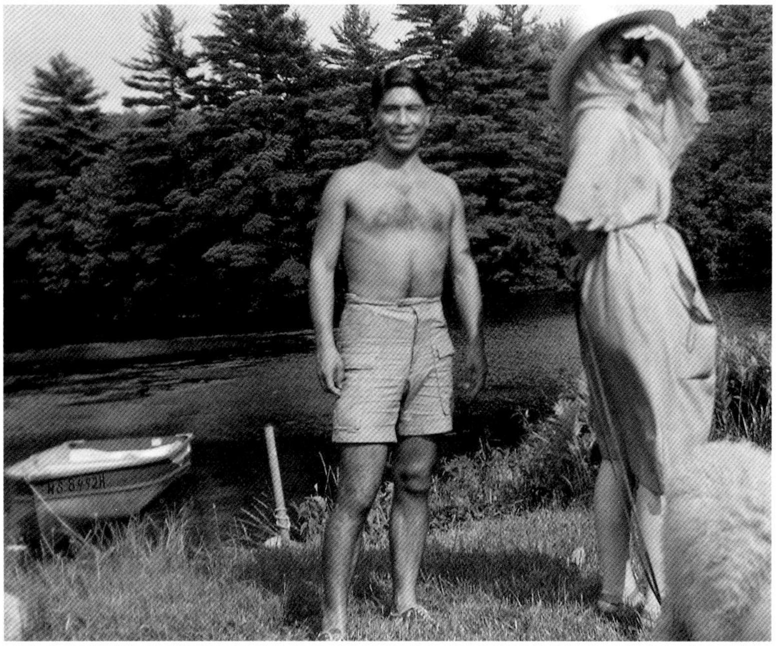

Fig. C.
Lois Orswell and Jaime Andrade
at Bafflin
Photograph by David Herbert
Estate of David Herbert
Collection of Jaime Andrade

SNAPSHOTS, POSTCARDS, TELEPHONE BILLS: THOUGHTS ON ARCHIVES AND HISTORY

IN A TIME WHEN SO MUCH OF OUR COMMUNICATION is made up of the electrical impulses that comprise e-mail and voicemail, it can be easy to forget that correspondence once left physical traces. Yet there was a time when not only the content but also the form of a letter conveyed information. Letters written or typed on paper reveal the process of composition; strikeouts and erasure marks give evidence of the changes and second thoughts that are eradicated by the delete button when a letter is composed on a computer. The correspondence of David Smith and Lois Orswell is particularly rich in this kind of information, with layers of meaning in even a brief postcard, conveyed by text, punctuation, placement, and commentary from the recipient.

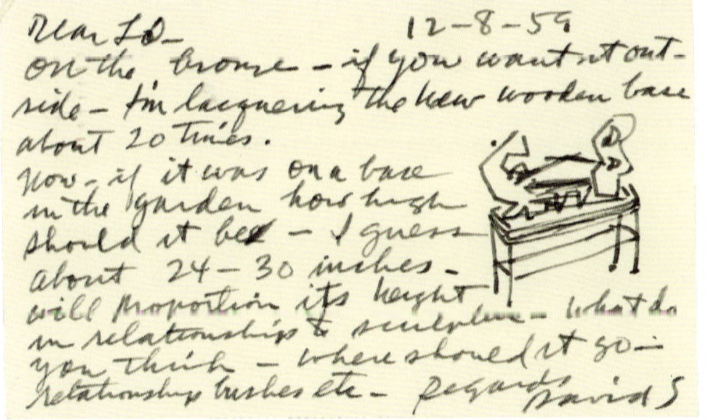
Dear LO— 12-8-59
on the bronze — if you want it out-
side — I'm lacquering the new wooden base
about 20 times.
now — if it was on a base
in the garden how high
should it be — I guess
about 24 — 30 inches —
will proportion its height
in relationship to sculpture — what do
you think — where should it go —
relationship bushes etc — Regards
David S

Fig. D.
Postcard from David Smith to Lois Orswell concerning the base for *Terpsichore and Euterpe*, dated 8 December 1959

The preparation and publication of the Smith-Orswell correspondence have been among the most satisfying opportunities of my career thus far, but I fear that the printed version does not adequately express to the reader the experience of reading the original letters in the collections of the Estate of David Smith and the Harvard University Art Museums.[1] No published transcript can convey the immediacy of a note scrawled on a torn sheet of yellow legal paper. Without holding the letter in one's hand, how could one detect the faint smudges of black indicating that the artist had made a carbon copy of a seemingly informal note hastily written on studio letterhead? Nor can a reading of the published letters reproduce the contrast between Smith's letters to Orswell, and to all his other correspondents: the former are handwritten, the latter typed, most often by the clerical assistant whose paychecks are recorded in a ledger found elsewhere in the archives. The organization of the archives themselves can be illuminating as well. In the case of the David Smith papers, their arrangement reflects their hasty retrieval from Terminal Iron Works only weeks after the artist's death. Even after Garnett McCoy's organization of the Smith materials, one still finds the odd piece of correspondence interleaved with sketches, phone bills, and equipment manuals, suggesting the intermingling of these ongoing conversations with the artist's working life. Occasionally, this correspondence provides a surprising contrast to our assumptions about the gruff character of the artist, as in the case of the letter from a local teenager, thanking Smith for donating hamburgers and french fries to the "teen canteen." Like the physical qualities of the original letters, these discoveries are reserved for the researcher.

Ideally, one would read the Smith-Orswell correspondence in the context of all the artist's correspondence of the time, to determine whether the themes that dominate Smith's correspondence with Orswell are reiterated or contradicted by his correspondence with others. The collected correspondence of David Smith is a project that has yet to be undertaken, but response to the publication of *Lois Orswell, David Smith, and Modern Art* suggests that there is more to learn about even such a well-documented artist as David Smith.

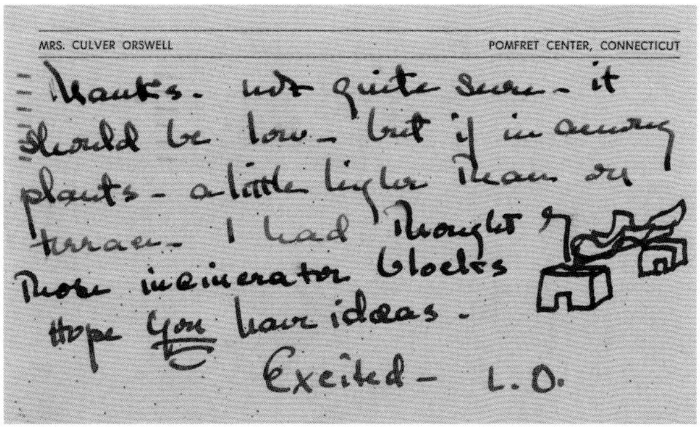
MRS. CULVER ORSWELL POMFRET CENTER, CONNECTICUT

Thanks. not quite sure - it should be low - but if in among plants - a little higher than on terrace - I had thought of those incinerator blocks Hope you have ideas - Excited - L.O.

Fig. E.
Postcard from Lois Orswell to David Smith concerning the installation of *Terpsichore and Euterpe,* postmarked 13 December 1959

Jaime Andrade's revelations about his interactions with both Smith and Orswell have especially fueled my curiosity in this respect. The letters and photographs he shared have contributed to our understanding of both the artist and the collector. Only recently, a catalogue stored in the Harvard University Art Museums' archives disgorged a letter from David Herbert to Lois Orswell, describing David Smith nervously observing the installation of his sculpture for the Marlborough-Gerson Gallery exhibition of 1964. This was a letter that could only be understood with the knowledge of the letters shared with us by Mr. Andrade. How many other individuals guard photographs, letters and memories that might offer us glimpses of the person behind the public persona of the artist?

So much of the history of art and its role in our culture and history lies not in the positioned, polished essay of the exhibition catalogue or the polemical journal article, but in the scrawled entries in a ledger, in the piles of receipts and ticket stubs not discarded. Archival sources can illuminate both the work of art and the world in which it was made, but only if they are made available to scholars.

Sarah B. Kianovsky
Assistant Curator of Paintings, Sculpture, and Decorative Arts, Fogg Art Museum

1. My access to the David Smith archives was facilitated by Peter Stevens, Rebecca Smith, and Candida Smith who have been unfailingly generous in allowing me to consult these materials. At the time that I began my research, the Smith archives (now maintained by the Estate) were housed in the Archives of American Art, whose staff offered me every courtesy a researcher could hope for. At the Harvard University Art Museums Archives, Abby Smith and Susan von Salis have cheerfully accommodated my frequent visits to look at the letters "one more time."

TO ANYONE INTERESTED:

Lois Orswell sent a letter to the director of the Fogg Art Museum in the summer of 1984 and enclosed a long statement about her relationship with David Smith. Although this statement is not a letter to the artist, it summarizes her longtime correspondence with him.

To any one interested:

There has been some slight interest shown in my acquaintance with David Smith and since he is one of the great artists of the century perhaps any small contribution to the knowledge of him would be welcome. . . During the early years I lived in Pomfret I resumed collecting to some extent though I did miss Curt Valentin whom I liked very much. I had wanted a Smith sculpture for years though my knowledge of his work was confined to photographs and what pieces I had seen at the Marion Willard Gallery which when I first knew it was next door to Curt Valentin. I decided suddenly that I simply must have some pieces and I had made no progress. I had gone to the last show he had with Willard and was a little taken aback by the new prices. This was the period of the simple strap-like pieces, all very vertical and the drawings were of that period also. I bought a drawing but no sculpture as I was not yet accustomed to pieces priced at $7000 which they all seemed to be. As a matter of fact David knew I had bought the drawing which he said was the only sale at that show. I telephoned Marion Willard and asked her if she had any pieces and she became almost hysterical. It seemed that David was leaving her gallery and she was distraught about it. Afterward he told me at great length he had not forgiven her because a sculpture had been stolen from her gallery. It happened to be the only hanging piece he ever made and I would love to have seen it. I often wonder if it ever came to the surface in these later years. Marion Willard told me after she calmed a little that she had just one piece left one called FLIGHT which was not at the gallery however but at Bolton Landing. I had seen the piece at a show at the Metropolitan and said I would take it.

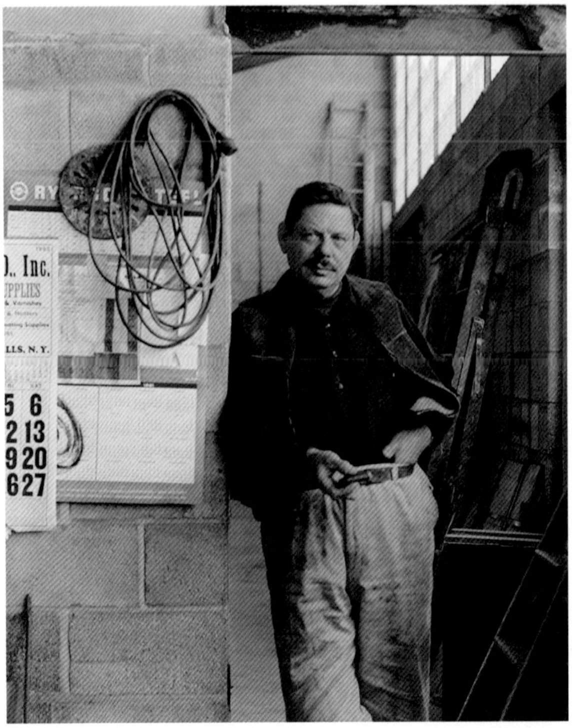

Fig. F.
David Smith
at Bolton Landing, 1962
Photograph by David Smith

I paid her a deposit and then got a high school boy who did chores for me after school to drive to the Landing with me. I was delighted of course to see an artist I had admired for so long and we had a very nice visit which had to be over night of course. We went to a motel run by an English couple named Brassington. When we collected the sculpture the next day and started off David said something about how was I paying for it and I explained I had made the purchase agreement with Willard so I had to send my check to her which I did. He took it with slightly bad grace as he rather pretended to be still irate at her. I always doubted he was quite as furious as he pretended but I do think he wanted to be taken seriously which he was not at that time. Of course one David Smith was not enough so later on I telephoned him and asked if I could come back. I forgot to say that the first time I went Jean was there and the two very young children. She was very pleasant and cordial but involved with babies and one had the impression that life was a bit hard and complicated. David was very possessive of her, possibly to the point of being dominating but then I am not sure from just that short visit. One thing was certain: he was thrilled with the two babies. It did not seem too long after that that Jean left and took the children with her but I do not recall quite how long. I think I had some dealings with him before that and he brought the GUITAR PLAYER here for me to try. Very stupidly I sent it back eventually as I found it difficult to mount. I am cross with myself for doing such a thing. Anyhow, when Jean did leave David was like a lost soul. He wandered about the country, back and forth to the Cape to see the Motherwells and goodness knows where else. One day I returned from a day away and found a drawing tucked into the handle of the front door. The message he left was sad and the drawing seemed very sad too. Another time he stopped through with a new rather old second hand Mercedes stayed to talk with a guest I had and then went off quite late. . . The next time I went to look at sculptures he was sadly living in bachelor quarters. . When I mentioned that I would have to look for a motel he said "Don't you dare stay in the same house with me?? are you afraid to??" And naturally I said Oh no of course not, but secretly wondering how scandalous it WOULD look but I decided with his friendly attitude I had no business being silly and Victorian. So one time I slept on the big leather sofa in the living room, I think that was the time when the girls were there with a sort of governess and David made a delicious dinner with lobster and big pickles he made himself. One time when the girls were not there he got out with great pride the special sheets he bought for them and made me up a bed in their room. It was very touching for he talked of them all the time he was working and showed with pride the girls drawings on the walls. The last time I went I curled up in the middle of his bed - as I remember it was big and bumpy with a black cover on it - and he slept on the leather sofa in the living room. The truth was by the time I curled up on those nights I could have slept on the floor. I left home usually just before dawn and got to Lake George about time for a lunch at a Johnson's (I think) and then going on to the Landing. When I arrived David would be working and he did not want to stop so I would have to think of something to do until he finished. I usually drove about, one day driving as far as Ticonderoga and back. By dinner time I was tired and hungry and then was the time to begin talking about sculpture and looking. By eleven or so when I was really weary David would be just warming up after one of his stock of Cuban cigars and he would begin opening up the enormous cabinets of drawings or climbing over the sculptures in the basement. How I ever really decided WHAT I wanted I do not know. One night I said I would like to see a certain bronze with the rain on it and I wonder now if I was just too sleepy to know what I was doing. But David very nicely put the big piece outside and poured a pail of water over it and there it was. Sometimes I brought the pieces home in my wagon I think the QUEEN came in my car but once he brought a piece - the FISH - in his truck and once he had some trucking firm deliver. Twice on the way home I went into Rutland and stopped at the marble quarry and loaded on some tall pieces for pedestals. That was quite a load but the marble was not successful. It was very heavy to handle and it tipped over and broke into pieces.

As I said after Jean left David was a sort of lost soul and he said he had to keep moving as he could not bear to stay at home. One Christmas during this time I was startled to hear from him. [*The year was 1959.*] He invited himself and fortunately I did have some food in the house. It was before I had my new kitchen so I was rather cramped but I remember I cooked a chicken, what else I cannot remember. I always have spent Christmas here alone which I prefer but during the time I had to have a "house sitter" staying in the guest house it was more festive. Anyhow at that time David spent the night in the guest house and the next morning I cannot remember how the subject of guns came up. I mentioned an old revolver I had that my mother had kept with her when we moved about and I said I had never dared shoot it. He told me it was time I did and loaded it up and made me go out with him and practice. What the people in the nearer houses thought to hear me shooting on Christmas morning I cannot imagine and of course cared less. David loaded the gun for me and those same shells are still in it. My house sitter was a strange person who had been sent to me sight unseen. He was what Henry James called a mythomaniac, he had a great store of wonderful stories about well known people all of which were suspect, the stories I mean. It was fun to listen to these two talk. David was a very interesting person in conversation, he was surprizingly well read and always had lots of ideas about projects, right down to rigging up a thing in his Franklin stove chimney to smoke meat. His attitude toward animals especially wild ones I took exception to but never let our opinions arrive at a row. But his chief interest was his daughters and what he wanted for them. When I was acquiring his sculpture he asked why I was doing it and what the ultimate disposition would be. I assured him that it would all go to Fogg and he said splendid and he would help me do it. He hoped the girls would go to Radcliffe. . He was at that time bitter about museums and I suppose he had reason and perhaps it was beyond reason but looking back they DID miss such a chance to acquire large numbers of his works. I think at that time MOMA had just one. They later gave him the one man show but did not buy any as I remember. What a chance to buy dozens! Cleveland asked him to donate a piece as they "had no money" which he refused for they were purchasing paintings at very high prices. Some museum in the West, I cannot remember where, something like Kansas City or St Louis or even Oklahoma had removed the colour from a sculpture and he was having a running fight about that. He was the first or almost to use colour on metal sculpture and the critics had made a great fuss about it way back during the Marion Willard period. I often think of how he felt about that museum when I hear that Clement Greenberg whom he trusted has had the surface changed on some things. I just know he would not have forgiven it. . . For a time David was on very close friendly terms with Anthony Caro and Kenneth Noland and I think Noland's painting influenced David's work for a time. That seemed strange as he was such a strong character it would seem strange for him to be influenced by any one. It lasted a short time however. I suppose those pieces I liked the least of his work and yet they do stand the passage of time very nicely.

The invitation to Italy was the great event in David's life and what fruit it did bear. He did not even know the name properly of the place he was going as he told me it was a place called BOLTRI., which turned out to be VOLTRI. The last time I went to the workshop he had been unpacking the material he brought back and there were rows upon rows of new pieces made from the objects he brought back.

His workshop was always a place of great fascination to me but I tried to be careful not to appear to be invasive for it was a very special and rather private place for him in spite of all the lifts. His assistant whose name I forget was a very nice person. I did one day ask if I could have some of the sketches stuck on the walls and reluctantly he allowed me to take some. They are the ones now framed up together at Fogg. These seemed to be about as close to the creative act of the artist as one could get. David was rather surprized at my interest in his painting which he took very seriously. He knew no one approved of it and was reluctant at first to let it go. But I wanted the COMPLETE artist. The spray paintings kept him interested at just the time he was the most depressed and he arrived once with a bundle of the long narrow canvases. Later at the studio I saw them framed and liked them. I think it was at that Christmas but I cannot remember, anyhow he brought the ones I have and one he installed himself in the room by the fireplace. He asked for long nails and a hammer and nailed one up over the windows. I had steel girders in the room I built for large paintings and he suggested I place the others along those girders which I did. It is interesting to note that he thought of all of them as hanging horizontally. When I went to the recent show at Fogg I was so surprized to see them all in vertical position but of course they had no way of knowing . . . The diversity and the quantity of work that he stored away in cabinets in his studio was incredible. And he was a man of wide interest and understanding. It must have taken ages to sort it all out and what an inheritance for the girls he loved so much.

At one time a friend in New York had asked me to write to Blanche Ribicoff as she had recently moved to Hartford. Which I did but never had a response. Very much later I was in a gallery at the Athenaeum and she spoke to me and mentioned my letter which she had not answered. After that she said she had heard I knew David Smith. I agreed I had been up to his studio to purchase some things and went on to say how devoted to and how he missed his girls. She listened, I felt, rather impatiently and then looked slightly furious and said firmly "Well THAT is not the way I heard that it is. I have heard dreadful things etc etc" . . And I just as firmly said I was sure she had but for me THAT WAS THE WAY I SAW IT. and it was. For me, David became a loyal friend and a most understanding one. I think he understood my character better than I did and he treated me accordingly. I was not a multimillionaire and he knew it but he also knew I was devoted to his work and he appreciated that. He made it just as easy as possible to acquire his work as he could when he needed the money the worst way. I think once I divided my payment into two relays but I made it a point to pay him carefully and promptly. It is good to be trusted, in one's judgement and in one's financial dealings, it happens not very often but I know David did trust me and I appreciated it. I certainly was deeply in earnest about his work and I think those trips to get it were about the best thing I ever did. . . Then toward the last David said he was about to sign up with Marlborough gallery having been visited several times by the famous Mr Lloyd. He said he knew I would not be able to afford their prices so he would wait until I had what pieces I wanted. Nothing could be more generous. I did want so much one of the big stainless steel pieces but he said he must have $30,000 for one. At that time my income was about half of what it is now and I did not quite dare do it. IF ONLY I HAD!. The show at French and Company had not sold one piece, and he did need to get better prices. He had one vague suggestion from a shopping center in Toronto for a stainless piece but that was all. So I could not keep him waiting for ever and with the purchase of the larger lost wax bronze I said all right I was finished. This piece I think looking back is my most favourite piece. I love it. He had been treating it with rhubarb juice from his garden to get the green surface and he was still treating it so he asked me to leave it behind and come back later for it. That was the last time I saw him. [*the year was 1963.*] I persuaded my dear friends from Barrington Carleton and Madeline Goff to go with me. Carleton drove us up we spent the night at a local motel and the next morning we went to see David and get the sculpture. Carleton took some wonderful slides of the things all outside where they were the most content and also a good snap of David himself. Sometime later I had a letter from David that was such a sad letter I could not bear it. I telephoned him and he said —"if you will come up I will give you a drawing." I said you need not give me anything but I will come. . I tarried a bit I am sorry to say but I was packing my overnight bag when I had the news of his death. Hilton Kramer rang up and he said he had one of those sad letters also and we were both very sad together over the long distance. I think we both had the same intuition about it all. Some years later on the QEII I spoke with Tatiana Lieberman and she can be very moving. She said quite frankly what SHE knew happened and I gripped her hand and dropped a few tears and said I had never really dared to speak openly about it.

Whatever any one thinks or knows or thinks he knows about David is immaterial to me. I only knew him as a kind and loyal and understanding friend and incidentally as an unusually loving - but perhaps eccentric - father to his daughters. That is all I need. David was loyal to his other friends. He particularly remembered John Graham. I mentioned once I had been looking at some of Graham's drawings and he said he would make a bargain with me: if I bought two of the drawings and gave them to Fogg he would add some of his own drawings. Which we did. I kept them all here for a time and then after David's death I took the Graham drawings and those David gave me at that time and gave them for David Smith. Also the sheaf of sketch pad drawings he made me promise to send nowhere but Fogg I also saw carefully that was where they went. He was loyal to me and I intended to be equally so to him. . Now all I owned is at Fogg and I am at peace about it and I do pray he is.

I am sure he is being grumpy and ornery and probably profane somewhere but he is also seeing beauty. . I wonder if the bathroom is still there with the pink fixtures and the green ones that he arranged because the girls could not decide what colour. . . . .

Lois Orswell—
7-28-84 [*signed and dated*]

Notes on reading foregoing:

The FLIGHT which was my first purchase was bought just when David was most furious at museums. He gave me orders to install it in cement and if asked to loan it to say it was impossible. Both of which I did dutifully and when it went to Fogg it had to be excavated from the cement. I think other artists felt that way at that time, very few museums dared buy Smiths or Nevelsons for instance.

Not only lobster but shrimp were his specialty in cooking and one evening he made an enormous skillet full of shrimp and garden herbs and Oh lots of oil and it was rather a heavy but delicious dish! When I was there he did not drink too much and usually had one of the Cuban cigars for dessert.

While I was waiting for David to be free I had a chance to look at the sculptures arranged on that beautiful hill and also half finished ones in the workshop. The one I bought called 5 1/2 I saw leaning against the building in just plain steel but I was sure I wanted it and after I said so he added that lovely surface which is on now. He told me it was "a very intimate piece to be near to one" which proved to be the case. I always had it next a large chair I often curled up in.

At one time there was a table in the workshop with great sheets of silver on it. Imagine leaving those about now. He began using silver after being asked by one of the table silver companies to make a small sculpture along with other sculptors. I wonder what happened to those.

David and I found we had one thing in common in our lives - his seeming to me rather boisterous and hectic and mine quiet and boring - and that was our Methodist mothers. I said every so often I would feel the Methodism catching up to me try how I might to forget it and he said "that is not the worst part which is being afraid it is creeping up on one without being aware of it".

David never forgot Margaret Brown a courageous small gallery owner in Boston. As she told me David "and a cute little girl both very much in love" stopped at the gallery on their way home from somewhere and they were completely out of money. She bought a drawing and that saved the day. I thought of that when I knew him and he was having an entire drawing show framed at his own expense by request of Sam Wagstaff at the Hartford Athenaeum. When the show was over Sam bought. . . just one drawing. . .

ON LOIS ORSWELL AND DAVID SMITH

THREE CONVERSATIONS WITH
MARJORIE B. COHN, HILTON KRAMER, AND JAIME ANDRADE

E.A. CARMEAN, JR.
SUMMER 2003

"My sculpture and especially my drawings, relate to my past work, the 3 or 4 in progress and to the visionary projection of what the next sculptures are to be."[1] So wrote David Smith, in words that might have come from his correspondence with Lois Orswell. In fact, Smith's thoughts were written in 1953, three years *before* their friendship began over her purchase of the sculpture *Flight* (1951) and an untitled drawing (of 1953).[2]

In meeting Lois Orswell – with her *own* interest in the artist's process[3] – Smith found the patron he must have been looking for; and, with his untimely death in 1965, Mrs. Orswell stopped looking for new art, and her collecting (already in financial hiatus) ended.

To further understand this unique artist/patron/museum relationship, I asked to interview three of Lois Orswell's friends. Marjorie B. (Jerry) Cohn, is the Acting Director of the Harvard University Art Museums and the Carl A. Weyerhaeuser Curator of Prints at the Fogg, and in many ways, her friendship with Lois Orswell assured that "the Orswell collection is at Harvard."[4] Her essay on Mrs. Orswell in the catalogue/book for the Fogg's exhibition is a model of biography, art history, and clarity.

Jerry's insights join those of Hilton Kramer. The distinguished art critic first at *Arts Magazine* and *The New York Times*, now at *The New Criterion*, the journal he founded twenty-five years ago (Lois Orswell was a fan), Kramer was uniquely a friend to both the artist and the patron.[5] From a third perspective, we have the memories of Jaime (Jimmy) Andrade of Knoedler & Company, who is profiled here by Ann Freedman in her "Salute." I only add that in knowing Jimmy for over thirty years, he indeed lights up a room with his presence.

As noted above, I originally intended more formal interviews with this "Orswell trio." But, in every case, their insights on Smith and his patron were matched by an enthusiasm for Lois Orswell the person. These infectious celebrations and recollections transformed our exchanges into conversations. And further, given that Mrs. Orswell was a private person, her having such wise and vibrant friends tells us even more about David Smith's extraordinary patron.

E. A. Carmean, Jr.

1. David Smith, in E.A. Carmean, Jr., *David Smith* (exh. cat.) (Washington D.C.: National Gallery of Art, 1982) p. 63.

2. For the correspondence, knowingly collected, edited, and annotated by Sarah B. Kianovsky, see "The Lois Orswell/David Smith Correspondence," in *Lois Orswell, David Smith, and Modern Art* (exh. cat.) (Cambridge: Harvard University Art Museums, 2002), especially p. 217 [hereafter *LODSMA*]. For some measure of Orswell's pioneering collecting, her purchase of the Smith drawing was the only sale in the artist's 1956 exhibition at the Willard Gallery. In the same way, her earlier purchase of two small Franz Klines on paper in 1950 represented the only sales from his first Egan Gallery exhibition.

3. "For LO direct from the wall," as inscribed by Smith on a drawing Orswell wanted from his studio, see Marjorie Cohn in *LODSMA*, p. 142.

4. James Cuno, *LODSMA*, p. 7.

5. "Hilton is a fine writer," Smith wrote to Orswell on 26 June 1961, in *LODSMA*, p. 261. About Kramer's "Lachaise and Others: The Orswell Collection," *Arts Yearbook* 4 (1961) pp. 87–100. The only other profile of her collection was fourteen years earlier, in Aline B. Louchheim's "Narragansett Novitiate," *Art News* 46:3 (May 1947).

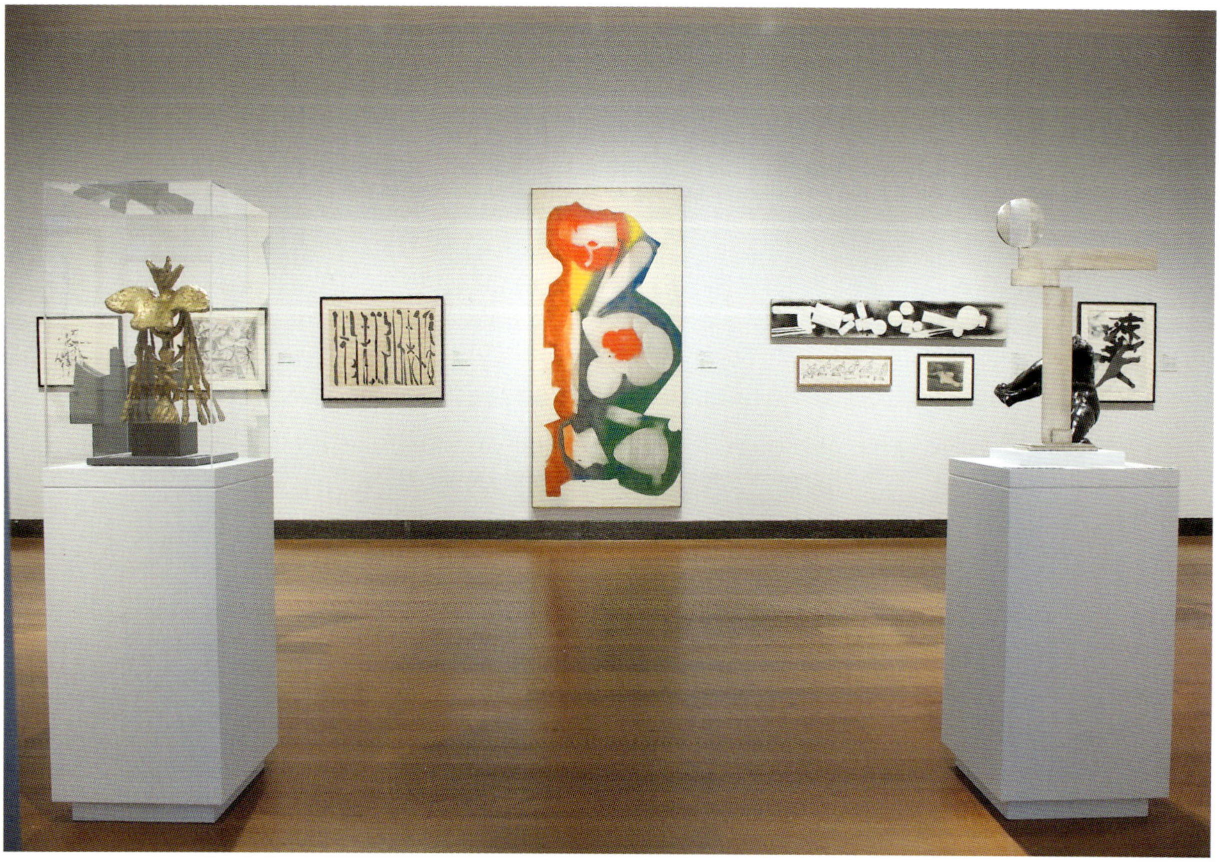

Fig. G. View of the exhibition *Lois Orswell, David Smith, and Modern Art*
Fogg Art Museum, Harvard University, September 21, 2002 – February 16, 2003

A CONVERSATION WITH MARJORIE B. COHN

EACJR.: *In your excellent art history essay and biography in* Lois Orswell, David Smith, and Modern Art, *you quote* LO *as saying "you know me: passionate and obstinate,"*[1] *and describe her "modesty and generosity," and cite Carleton Goff on the "pride she felt in her own perceptiveness. . . ."*[2] *How did these come together in the person?*

MC: There was not a single characteristic . . . not a single set. She had her own understanding of things. I can give you an example from the Gulf War – the first Gulf War [1992]. In speaking with her, it was as if she had *integrated* her knowledge about it. *Her* concerns were about the destruction in the oil fields and the effects the oil spills would have on the environment: I know she gave money to support efforts to protect the wildlife. And, in talking about it, I have no idea how she felt about the war itself, although my guess is that she supported it, that she was politically conservative. It was her conclusions that she expressed.

It could be a jolt in seeing that: For her – she was not content to just consider, but she would think through and express only conclusions. She had very strong convictions about the arts – not only what she collected, but also music and literature and this was unusual; most people in the visual arts are not so attuned to the other arts. And LO had extreme opinions about novels and music – and they could be very sophisticated and eccentric. She had a high level of knowledge about all three areas; she had studied music when younger[3] and was talented even in older age. And in her house there were books everywhere, piled seven, ten high (she was delighted, in her late years, she could order by mail). On a personal level, she otherwise led an austere life . . . not an intellectual life.

EACJR.: *LO was unique in her focus on sculpture, not only in attending to the medium itself, but in her collecting in-depth. One of the under-explored areas of early modern art in the U.S. is the number of very talented women who were sculptors.*

MC: That's right – including Katherine Weems, Anna Huntington, Malvina Hoffmann.

EACJR.: *In this context, I'm curious about Charlotte Jordan – whom you profile in your discussion of* LO *– and especially because Charlotte Jordan was also a sculptor.*

MC: As I wrote in the book, LO certainly acknowledged Charlotte Jordan – but on Jordan's *collection* being an influence, she did not have the same taste as LO.

Where there was a *strong influence* was with Curt Valentin [The Buchholz Gallery], who shaped and expanded her taste. But . . . how did she focus on sculpture? In the 1940s, LO did not have a lot of money and paintings were expensive – it was probably cheaper for sculpture and certainly for drawings and prints; but LO did not collect prints. *[Marjorie Cohn gives an engaging account of the dialogue on the subject, between LO and herself – she was and is the curator of prints at the Fogg![4]].*

EACJR.: *In addition to Curt Valentin, did sculptor Jacques Lipchitz have any influence at this time?*

MC: Although she went to Lipchitz's studio, I'm not sure she knew him that well – that visit was more of a one-time thing.

EACJR.: *Back to Valentin . . .*

MC: It was still *her choice*. I know that when she went into Valentin's, she would look at *all sorts of things*. She would consider then what to do . . . it was her choice, she had seen it and studied it.

She might listen to a consultant, but she would have felt that it [collecting decisions] was to be done personally. That is also the way with her Asian art – she collected what *she* liked – heads, Buddhas, others. As she also did – she was close to – the Classical antiquities she collected – but sculpture, not Greek vase painting.

EACJR.: *And you quoted her comment about the Metropolitan referring to "the Classical section where I have many old friends."*[5]

This raises a question. You discuss her Gandharan Head of a Buddha, *and her delight – indeed, her "Field" – being the way in which the Gandharan* Head *is the fusion of Greek forms and the later-to-emerge vocabulary of India.*[6] *For to me, David Smith's art occupies a similar position – in many ways, Smith is the last great sculptor in the tradition from Greece through the Old Masters – and yet, his art directed sculpture's next directions.*

MC: In her collecting, of course, LO could go from one tradition to another. She read extensively about art, was informed. But, as for David Smith being part of the tradition of sculpture and also being new – she never said anything about that. But . . . *she would have loved it!* Those were the kinds of things she liked to think about. And that an important [Smith] scholar said this. . . . She would just *melt!*

In other ways, she was modest in the presence of "experts," she was often aware I was a "curator from Harvard" and we'd have to get around that.

EACJR.: *I have another, and perhaps odd, question . . . about the traditional architecture and the courtyard at the Fogg.*

MC: LO, of course, liked modern architecture – after all, she lived in a very modern house. But, you're right – she did have a connection to the Fogg and its building. I know that she was reluctant to give her Beckmann triptych [*The Actors*] because she did not want it shown at the Busch-Reisinger Museum *[now, with the Fogg, part of the Harvard University Art Museums]*; it was only after John Coolidge, then the director of the Fogg, assured her it would remain at the Fogg that she would complete the gift.

And, in a way this might be related to the big question of her collection coming to Harvard. She lived in Boston the year the Fogg opened, and I've often wondered if her commitment to the museum might be – romantically might date back to LO and her beau at the time possibly coming to the Fogg during its first days, during its opening.[7]

She would say very little about this. You had to be very careful with LO and never ask a direct question. . . . And if you asked the *wrong* question, she would just clam up . . . and wait . . . until *I* changed the subject.

EACJR.: *I asked the question [about architecture] also in relationship to her unparalleled collection gift of David Smith's works, and in particular, the idea of placing his sculpture in a "Classical" setting (which Smith realized in the Roman-era arena of his* Voltri *sculptures) . . . and we know from Sarah's [Sarah B. Kianovsky] thorough annotation of their correspondence that Smith sent to LO a copy of* Voltron,[8] *the book on the project. Perhaps I'm seeking to understand the background to the extraordinary aspect of LO's patronage of the Fogg and David Smith, and in that sense her vision of bringing them together – and, this occurring at a time when Smith was very anti-museum! In this regard, did Smith visit the Fogg?*

MC: We don't know. He never scheduled an appointment – and John Coolidge, who loved sculpture, would certainly have greeted him.

On the plans for her collection [including her 48 Smith works] to go to the Fogg, it wasn't until 1961 that she let David Smith in on it –

although I think he had the idea all along that it was going to a museum. And, as the correspondence shows, knowing of Harvard and the Fogg, he responded with ideas, his dreams of his daughters going to Radcliffe.

EACJR.: *[In conjunction with these conversations with Orswell's friends, I also discussed the collector with the artist Michael Goldberg, who visited her at Pomfret Center in 1956 (his* Untitled, *ca. 1956 is included in the Knoedler exhibition). Goldberg commented on the idea of Orswell's in-depth collection of Smiths going to Harvard and the Fogg: "It's the kind of thing Smith would have wanted. He was pretty much alone during the winter up there at Bolton Landing. He'd fix himself those elaborate dinners to counter the loneliness and I can picture him sitting there at night imagining what the collection should look like."]*

MC: But there was little time . . . because of his death and then the steep rise in prices. And even before that, LO needed *[for monetary reasons]* to restrain her collecting. I think he knew and welcomed what LO wanted to do – with his work – at the Fogg. When Smith clearly knew she couldn't afford one of his new *Cubi* sculptures – he tucked a drawing of one *[Cubi XXII]* into a package, as a gift to her . . . and to Harvard.

1. Undated letter from Lois Orswell to Marjorie B. Cohn, quoted in Marjorie B. Cohn. *Lois Orswell, David Smith, and Modern Art* (Cambridge: Harvard University Art Museums, 2002) p. 12.
2. Marjorie B. Cohn. *Lois Orswell, David Smith, and Modern Art* (Cambridge: Harvard University Art Museums, 2002) p. 177.
3. Ibid pp. 21–22.
4. Ibid p. 88.
5. Ibid p. 61.
6. Ibid pp. 162–163.
7. Ibid p. 23.
8. Ibid pp. 287–288.

A CONVERSATION WITH HILTON KRAMER

EACJR.: *Your historical position and perspective is unique, having been a friend of both David Smith and Lois Orswell, and perhaps especially Orswell, for she is usually described as a private person.*

HK: Lois was private, and she was adamant about her privacy. I believe that during all the years I knew Lois, I never saw her at a gallery or museum opening or any other art world event. Very few people in the New York art world knew her or knew that she was collecting, except the artists and the dealers.

EACJR.: *And yet, she did allow you to publish an article on her collection in* Arts *(in 1961)?*[1]

HK: She and I got along very well. . . . I think she wanted to do this [article] in part because of her concern with Gaston Lachaise being better known. By then, Lachaise had sort of disappeared. She felt that Lachaise would be given some visibility.

EACJR.: *As with David Smith later (and the Fogg), this reflected her commitment to the artist.*

HK: She was very selective in her collecting. There were artists whose works she disapproved of, but she didn't discuss them, [there was] no criticism of their work.

EACJR.: *In your* New York Observer *article on the Fogg exhibition, you wrote a remarkable description of your first meeting Lois Orswell up at Bolton Landing.*

> This was in the summer of 1957. I was spending a few weeks at Yaddo. . . . Smith lived and worked further north, just above Lake George, at Bolton Landing, where his studio, the Terminal Iron Works, was already something of a legend in the New York art world. When he heard that I was at Yaddo, Smith invited me to visit him and see his new work.
>
> On the day I arrived, Smith promptly announced that he was expecting another visitor that day – a "lady," as he said, who was coming to pick up a sculpture she was acquiring for her collection. I think it was *Flight* (1951). When the "lady" in question arrived a short time later – she had driven all the way from her home in Pomfret, Conn. – the figure who emerged from her fancy station

> wagon looked, to my eye, like something out of a portrait by John Singer Sargent, complete with beribboned, broad-brimmed straw hat and flowing, diaphanous garments shimmering in the summer breeze. She was gracious, respectful, amusing, and very smart; it didn't take long to discover that Orswell had a mind of her own and a will of iron.[2]

What were they like in their interactions?

HK: Lois was very animated when she was in David's presence and he was his gentlest in hers. They were both very different [from their other characteristics] when they were together.

EACJR.: *I have a many-part question about Smith and Orswell and her collection of his work going to the Fogg. I have the clear sense that Smith was concerned with the presentation of his sculpture – not only with his installing his work at Lois Orswell's house and garden, but in a specific, extraordinary instance when he sent you annotated photographs for your* Arts *article on his work.*[3]

HK: Many of his comments were about works not finished or not yet assembled on the studio floor; he wanted to make it clear he was still at work on them.

EACJR.: *Thank you . . . because I want to get to that – a question about Smith's interest in process – in a minute. Before that . . . something I've found unexplored is the appearance in the late 1950s or the early 1960s of the idea of the artist – the Abstract Expressionist – having a museum dedicated to their work, or in-depth collections. Rothko wanted his work kept together not only in the intended Seagram murals, but also and interestingly with the Harvard paintings; and in 1961 Motherwell wrote an article on "What should a museum be?" and cited Smith's sculpture fields as an example. Was this "in the air" at the time? Including Smith?*

HK: On this idea of the museum, I believe this really began in the 1960s. With Smith, the fields with his sculpture began in the 1950s simply because he had no other place to put it . . . his studio and house were small . . . so he put the sculpture outside. Of course, later – as they began to fill up, they became important.

EACJR.: *Not speaking only about Smith, it seems that during this time period (late 1940s to mid 1960s), Lois Orswell was unique in collecting sculpture and drawings?*

HK: Well, at this time there were others who might buy a sculpture and drawings related to it. But, yes, on the scale that Lois did it, first with Lachaise, then David Smith, there was no one like her.[4]

EACJR.: *And this returns to Smith's interest in process – what he called the "stream" of his art. In this context, the appearance of Lois Orswell and her in-depth collecting must have been extraordinary. And then, his knowing that Lois Orswell's collection of his work, in this form, was going to a museum . . . to the Fogg.*

HK: And . . . well, you know about his quarrel with museums, his attitude then about museums.

EACJR.: *Comment?*

HK: I can mention one experience that made his views clear. One day, David and I went to the Clark in Williamstown. Neither of us had been there before. We came into one of the galleries and it had a pair of those bronze stanchions [with a cord] in front of a painting. And he went over to one and pointed to it. He may have even picked it up. And started almost shouting, "Do you see this! Do you know what this thing costs! Do you know what sculpture they could buy for this money!?"

And we went into another gallery and there were more stanchions! And David grew louder! The guards were now watching us. I was sure we'd be asked to leave.

EACJR.: *But, regarding the Fogg?*

HK: I think he saw that with Lois and with her collection and with this particular museum . . . there was a bond.

1. "Lachaise and Others: The Orswell Collection," *Arts Yearbook* 4 (1961).
2. Hilton Kramer, "Stalwart Lois Orswell Allowed David Smith His Great Career," *The New York Observer* (February 17, 2003).
3. Kramer, Hilton. "The Sculptor David Smith," *Arts Magazine* 34 (February 1960), entire issue devoted to Smith.
4. Hilton Kramer: "There were others who bought a lot of one artist's work. I remember one who did for monetary reasons, who one Friday evening at a dinner came up and asked me, "You see a lot of young artists," — I was then at *The New York Times* — "so who should I buy?" I was so furious at even being asked the question, given my position, that I told him three names I just made up and he replied, "I already own their works." And I knew he would spend the next morning, a Saturday, calling dealers trying to find those [made-up] artists."

EACJr.: *You spent time with Lois Orswell at her house in Connecticut, as a weekend guest or summertime visitor. How would you describe her?*

JA: She was very polite and restrained and exacting – discreet. Her big poodle dogs were too! I remember I would be sitting in her house (Mrs. Orswell also had a guest house for visitors) and a dog would come in . . . and she had these *[hand gestures tall]* sculptures just standing on the table, on the coffee table, and they could easily fall over. I'd think the big dog would go by and bump the table or something and knock over a sculpture. . . . But it never happened! It was as if the dog knew not to touch – to be discreet!!

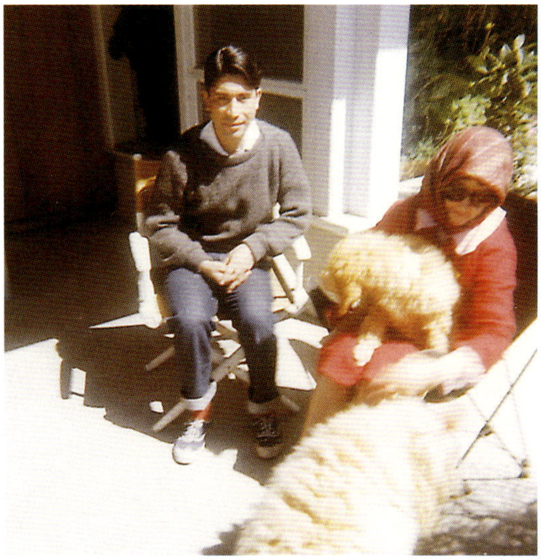

Fig. H.
Lois Orswell and Jaime Andrade at Bafflin
Photograph by David Herbert
Estate of David Herbert
Collection of Jaime Andrade

EACJr.: *Did you ever meet other collectors there – coming to see her collection?*

JA: No, but she knew other collectors whom I also knew. She would see them in New York. She knew Richard Brown Baker; they were both from Rhode Island and they would talk about art and their families.

She seemed to know everything. She would study books and read magazines – in English and in French.

EACJr.: *Lois Orswell was also very knowledgeable, well-informed about music; she had formal training in singing. Was music a part of your weekend visits?*

JA: She never had a record player, but there was a radio. Sometimes – to have music, I brought along my tape recorder, and we would go outside to listen . . . to "happy music."

EACJr.: *Happy music?*

JA: "Happy music" . . . Caribbean music. And I would play it and dance around in the garden.[1] Mrs. Orswell would come out and listen and start to move. She would ask me to show the dance to her and to others who were there. I would teach her the steps – the dance moves; I had studied with Martha Graham for six months when I first came to New York. She would learn the steps. Then I would play the tape recorder – the "happy music" — and we would all dance — dance around the garden, around the David Smith sculpture.

EACJR.: *Many collectors need to move works around when they buy a new picture or sculpture — or they might rearrange works to try new combinations. Did you ever see Lois Orswell do this?*

JA: I actually never saw things moved; some works might be in a different place from one visit to another, but never a David Smith. Where he had put a sculpture or a painting — he would always choose the place — it would not be moved. It was exactly where he put it.

EACJR.: *Did you ever meet Smith at Lois Orswell's?*

JA: Once, it was around 1963, and it was funny — later *[laughs]*. I went out to her guest house with her . . . and there was this big man with a big moustache and a big cigar. He was sitting there reading a book. She introduced me to him, and him to me as "David Smith." And he said, "Hello, Jimmy." But I didn't realize *[laugh]* he was David Smith the *artist*. I thought he was just a big man named David Smith, so I didn't pay too much attention to him *[laughs]*.

EACJR.: *How did they interact?*

JA: They were friendly and very polite with each other, a little formal. And, they talked about all kinds of things. She had opinions, but she would defer to him.

That was the only time I saw him there. He died in an accident sometime after this visit. It was then *[in 1965]* that she told my good friend, David Herbert,[2] that her entire collection was going to Harvard.

1. EACJr.: *On Orswell's energetic enthusiasm, Michael Goldberg (see also p. 28) recalled of his 1956 visit: "One thing I remember about her. She was, as I said, very restrained . . . very proper . . . until she got involved telling a story . . . talking about literature. Then she would suddenly become very active . . . her hands, arms would be moving around . . . almost acting out what she was describing."*
2. David Herbert (1925–1996) was a highly respected New York art dealer who began his career working for Betty Parsons and later Sidney Janis, before opening his own gallery in 1959. Lois Orswell was his client and close friend, and he introduced her to Jaime Andrade.

WORKS IN THE EXHIBITION

All works courtesy of the Fogg Art Museum
Harvard University Art Museums
Gift of Lois Orswell, except where noted

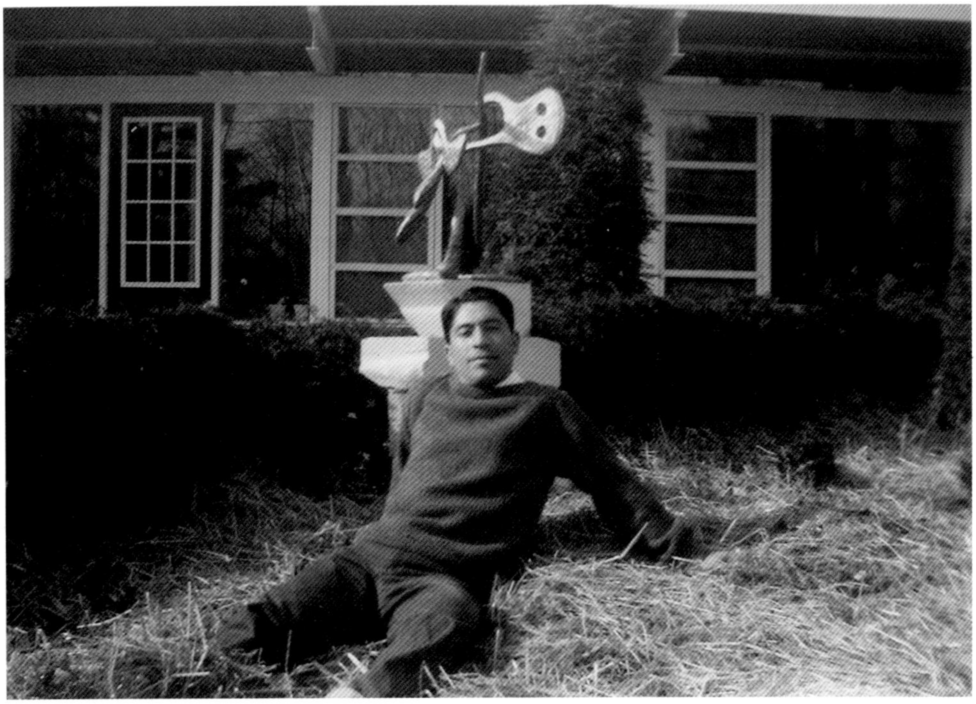

Fig. I.
Jaime Andrade at Bafflin with
Calder's *Octopus*
Photograph by David Herbert
Estate of David Herbert
Collection of Jaime Andrade

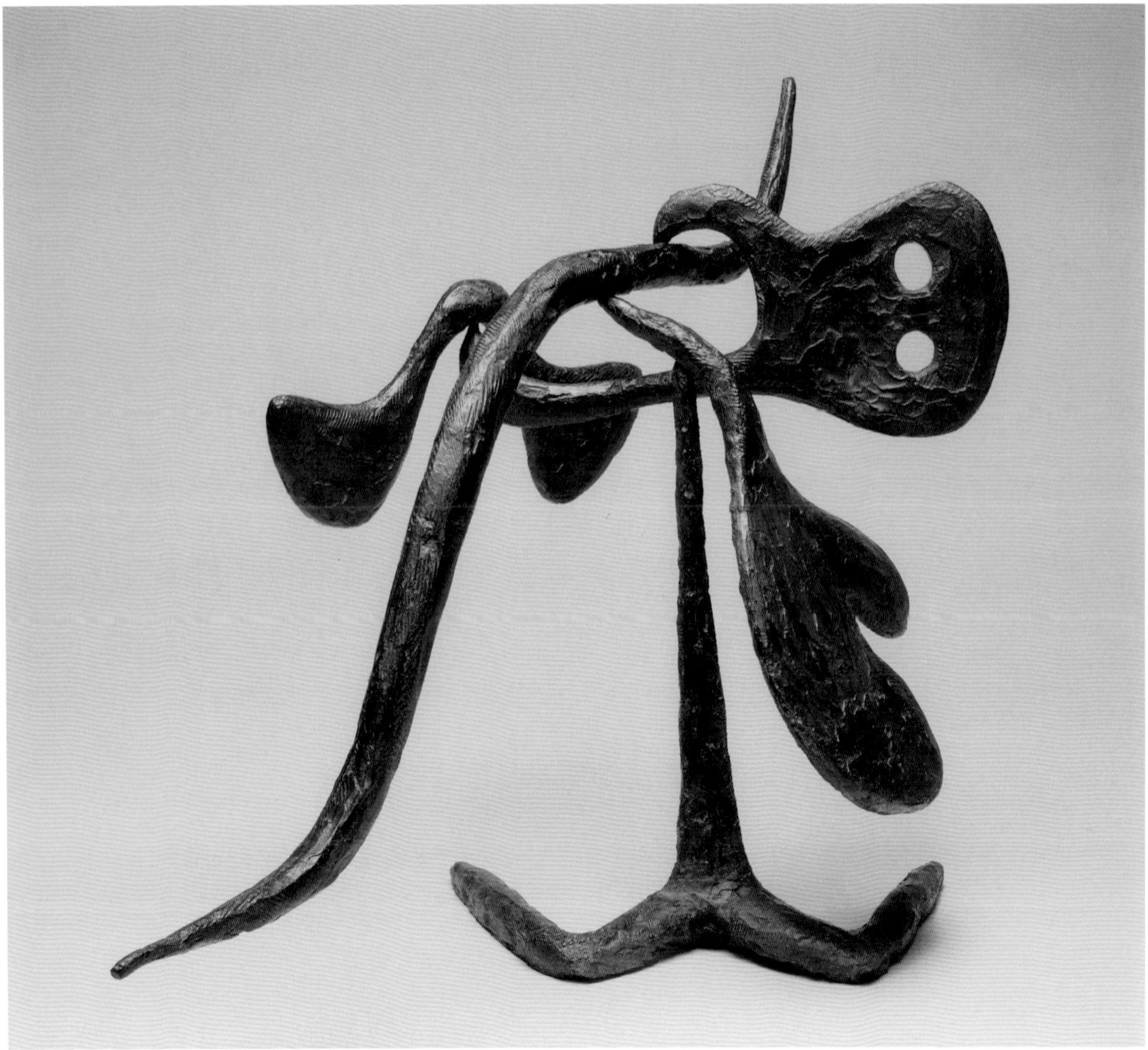

1. ALEXANDER CALDER
(1898–1976)
Octopus, 1944
Bronze
63.5 x 90.8 x 59.7 cm.

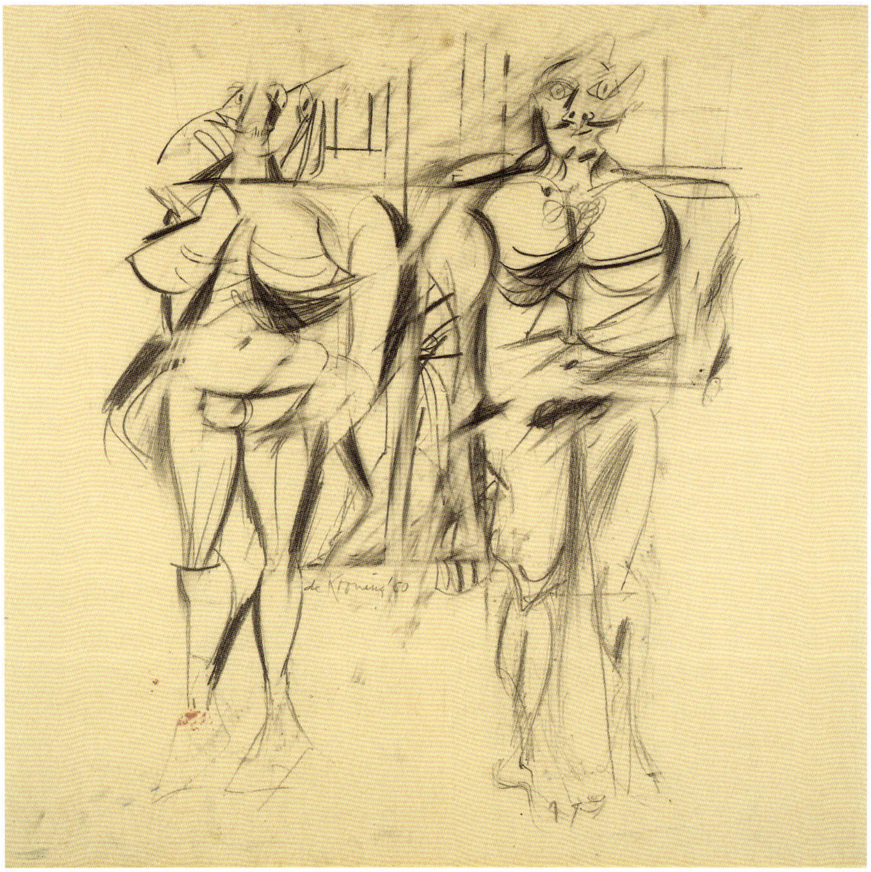

2. WILLEM DE KOONING
(1904–1997)
Two Nude Figures, 1950
Graphite and crayon on
heavy cream paper
40.8 x 56.1 cm.

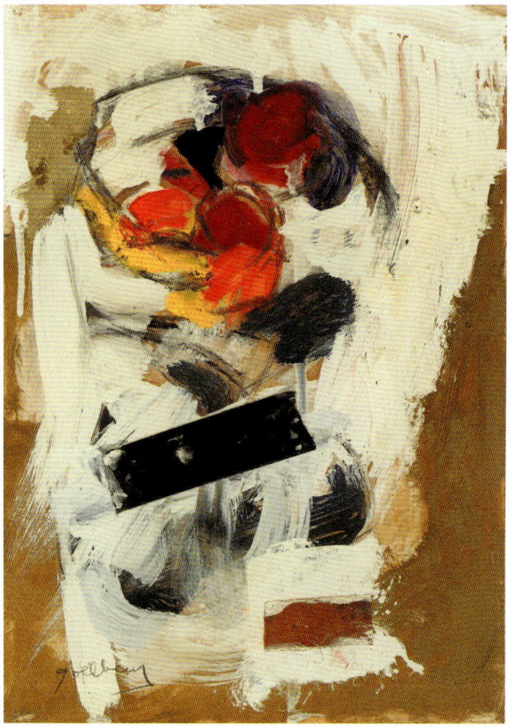

3. MICHAEL GOLDBERG
(b. 1924)
Untitled, ca. 1956
Oil paint, charcoal, and
pressure-sensitive-tape
collage elements on
wove paper
30.1 x 21.6 cm.

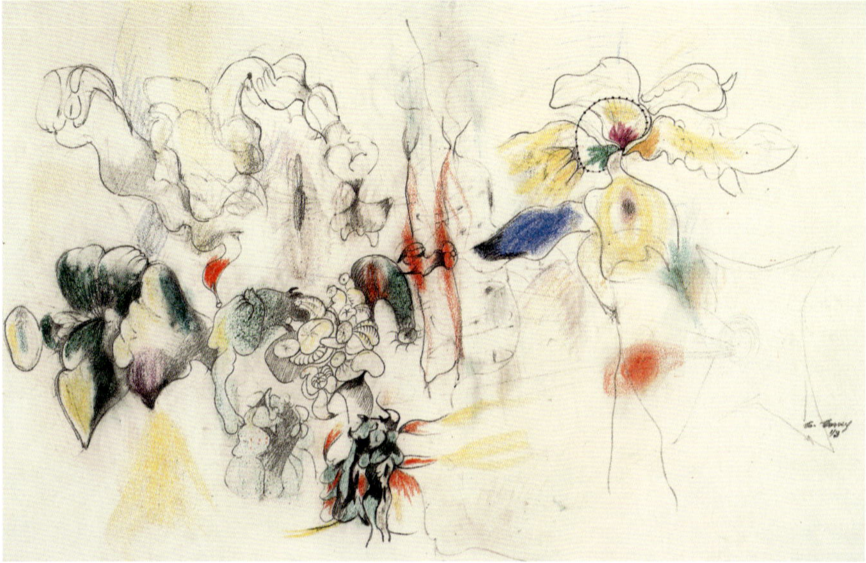

4. ARSHILE GORKY
(1904–1948)
Flowers, 1943
Graphite and colored wax crayon with extensive stumping, erasure, and working with a sharp tool on paper
35.4 x 56.4 cm.

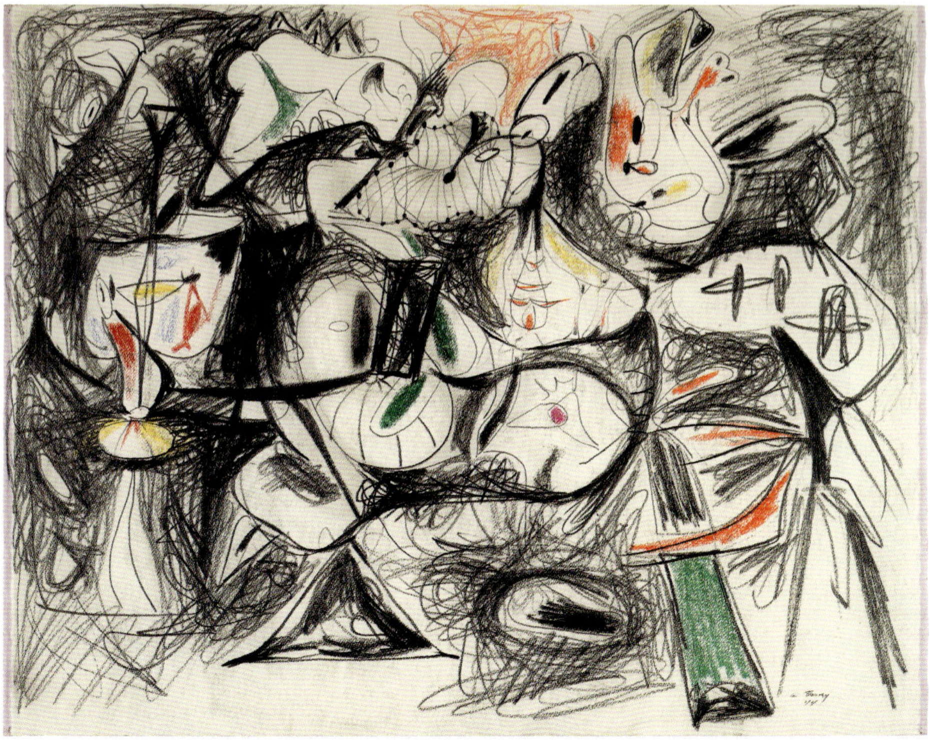

5. ARSHILE GORKY
Untitled, 1944
Graphite and colored wax crayon with stumping on off-white wove paper edged with lavender paper on left and right sides
50.7 x 66.2 cm.

6. ARSHILE GORKY
Untitled, ca. 1944
Two kinds of graphite and colored wax crayon with extensive stumping on off-white wove paper edged with lavender paper on left and right sides
50.5 x 66.2 cm.

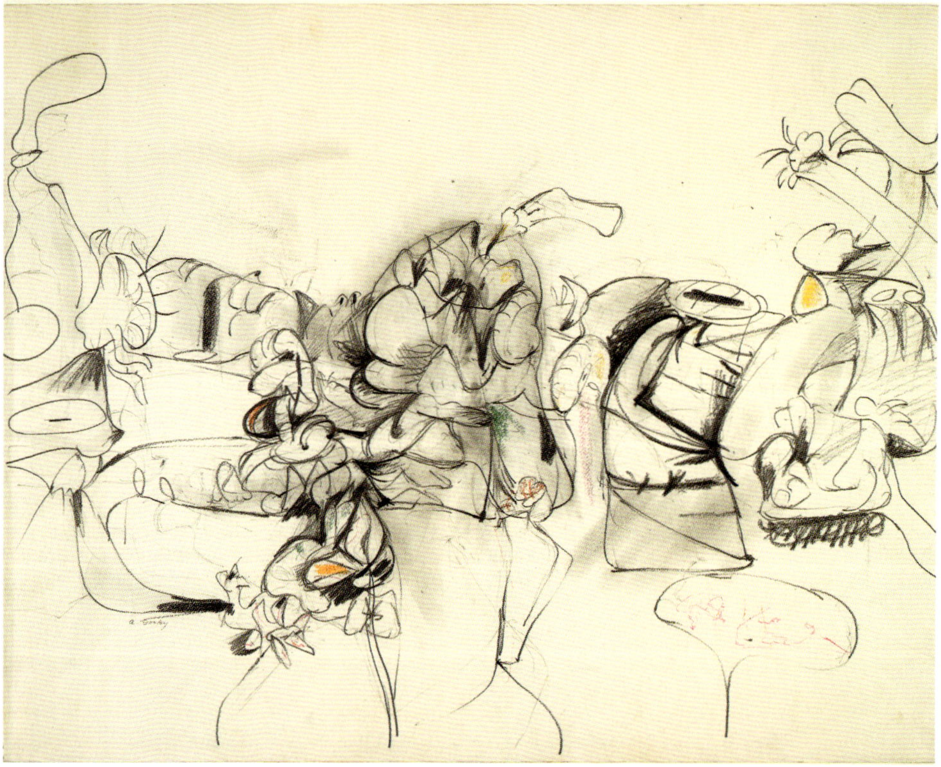

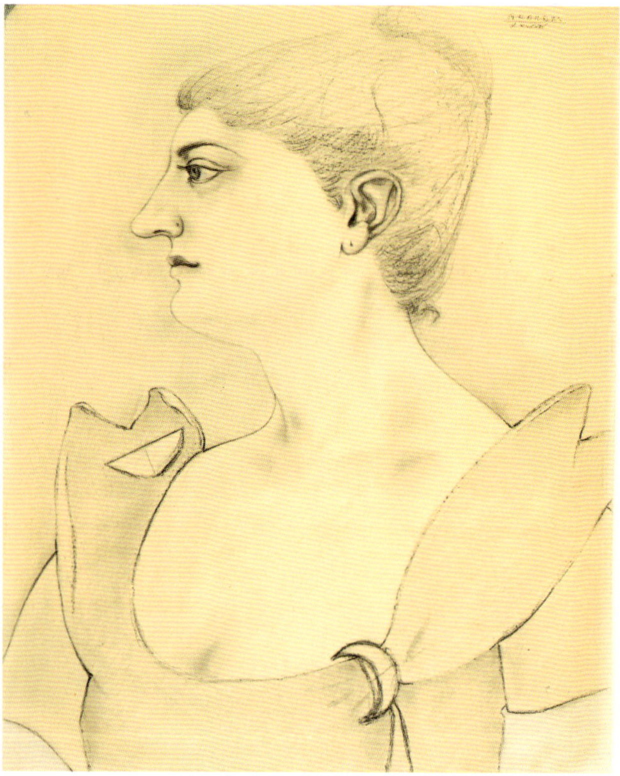

7. JOHN D. GRAHAM
(1886–1961)
Madame Sijou, 1944
Graphite and crayon on off-white tracing paper
60.6 x 48.0 cm.

Courtesy of the Fogg Art Museum, Harvard University Art Museums, Gift of David Smith in memory of his friend, John Graham

8. JOHN D. GRAHAM

Self-Portrait as a Warrior, not dated

Carbon paper transfer, graphite, and white chalk on cream wove paper

42.2 x 34.0 cm.

Courtesy of the Fogg Art Museum, Harvard University Art Museums, By gift, and purchase, Louise Haskell Daly and Francis H. Burr Funds

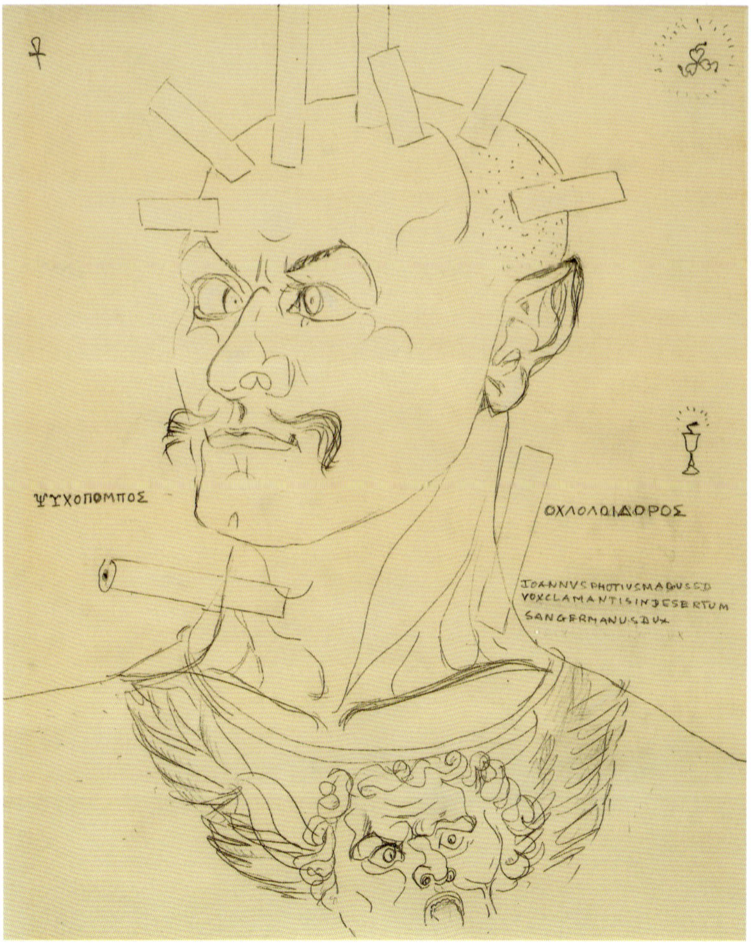

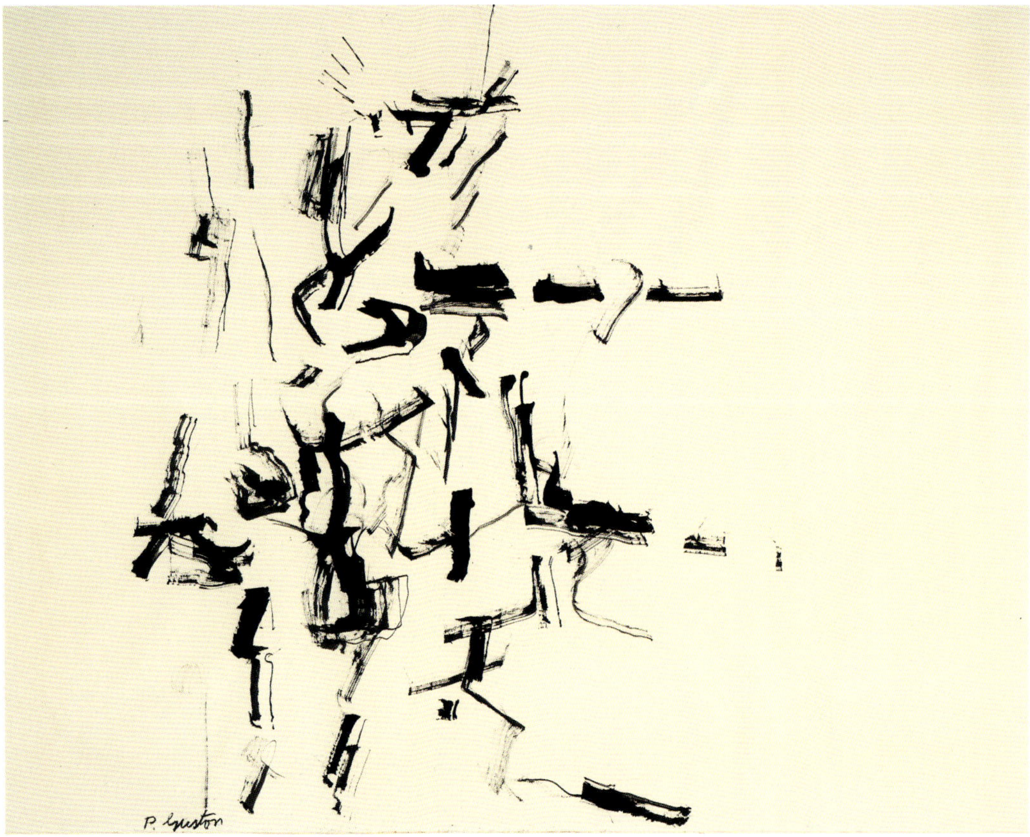

9. PHILIP GUSTON
(1913–1980)
Untitled, ca. 1953
Black ink on cream wove paper
45.5 x 60.9 cm.

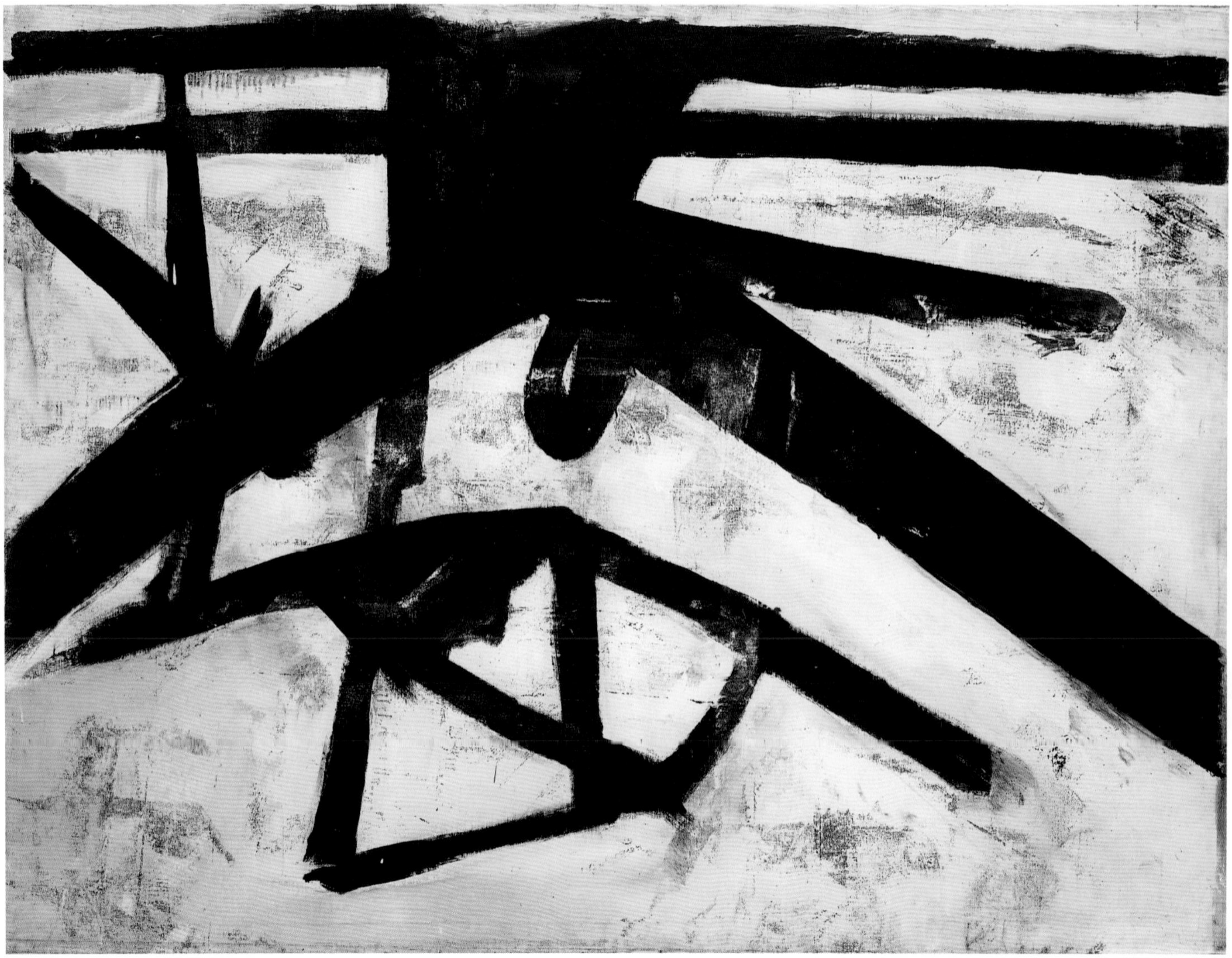

10. FRANZ KLINE
(1910–1962)
High Street, 1950
Oil on canvas
146.2 x 195.0 cm.

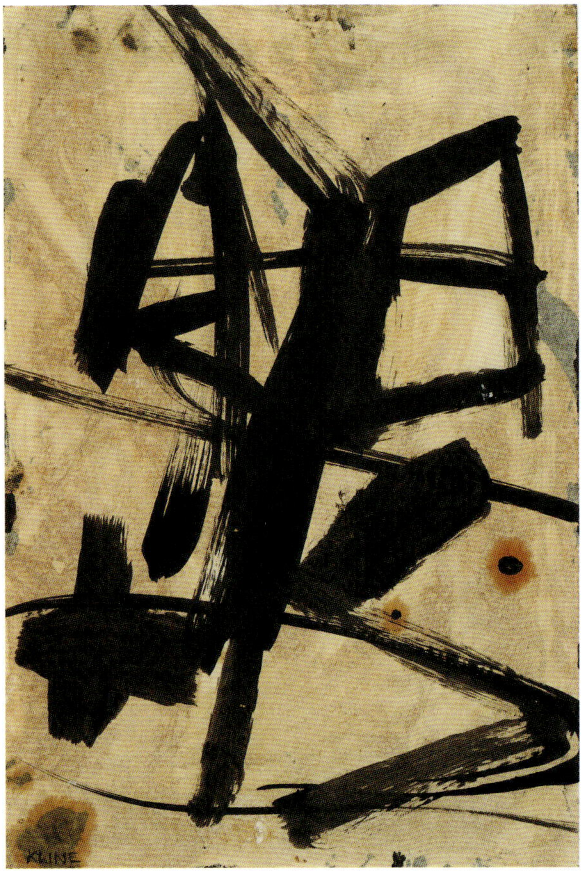

11. FRANZ KLINE
Untitled, ca. 1950
Black ink and oil paint on
thin off-white wove paper
mounted on ivory wove paper
26.6 x 18.3 cm.
Courtesy of the Fogg Art Museum,
Harvard University Art Museums,
The Lois Orswell Collection

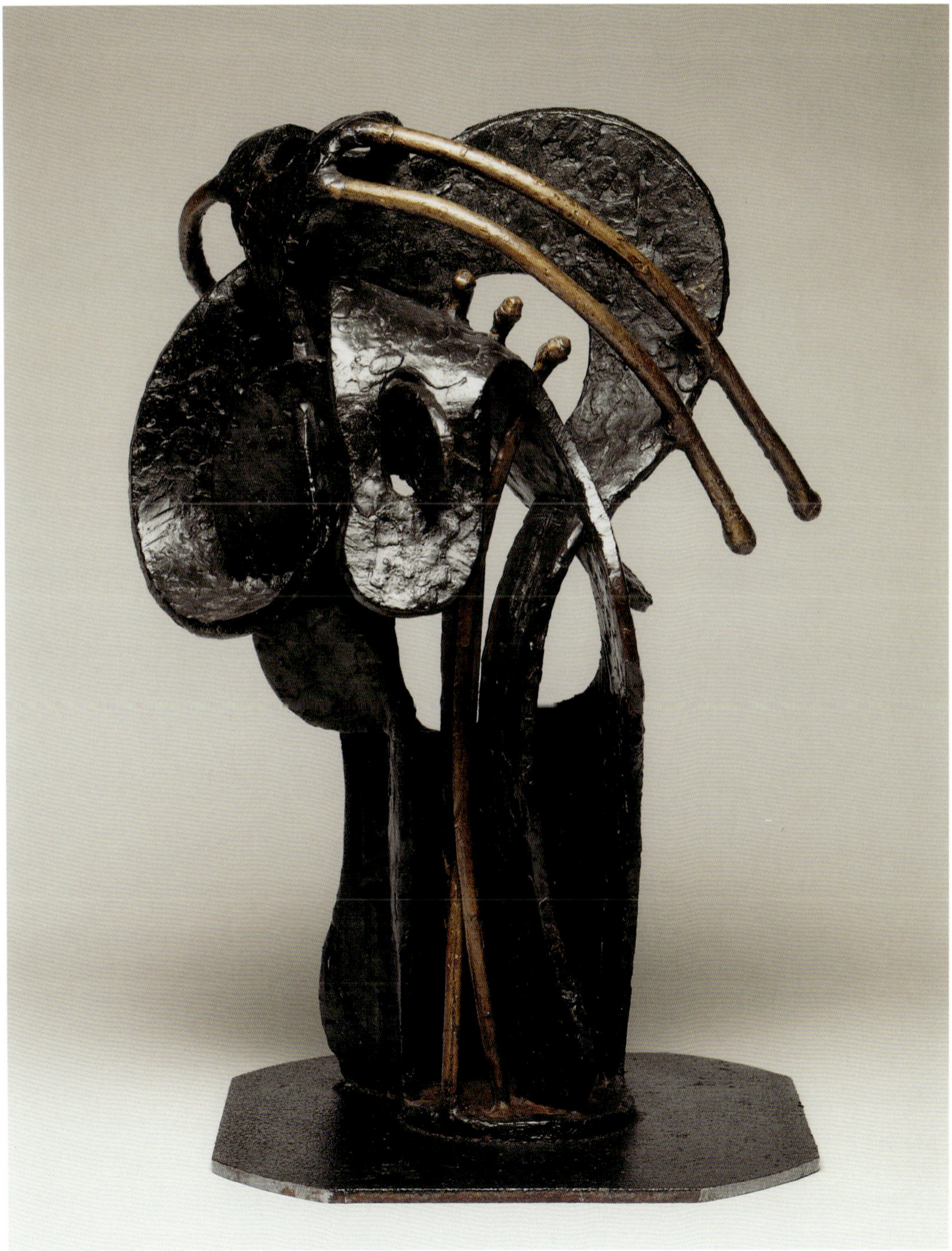

12. JACQUES LIPCHITZ
(1891–1973)
Trentina, 1946
Bronze with gold paint
52.2 x 32.0 x 31.0 cm.

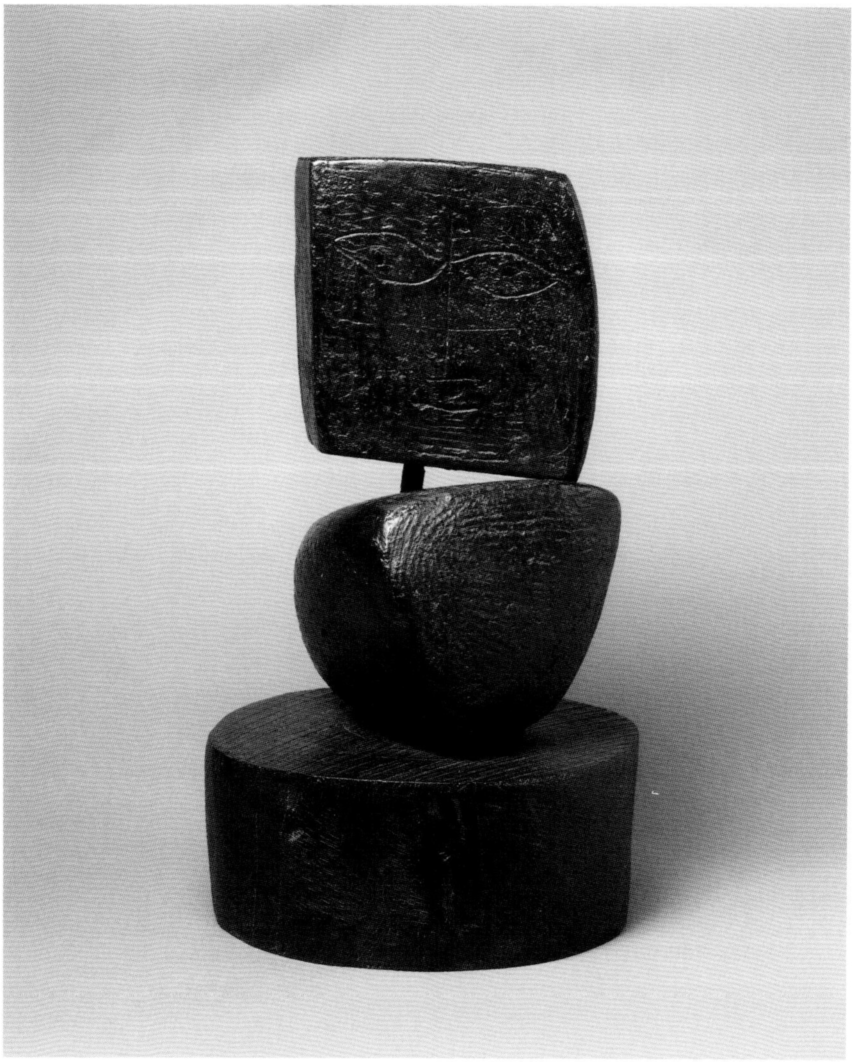

13. LOUISE NEVELSON
(1900–1988)
Figure, ca. 1947
Plaster with wood base
height: 31.1 cm.

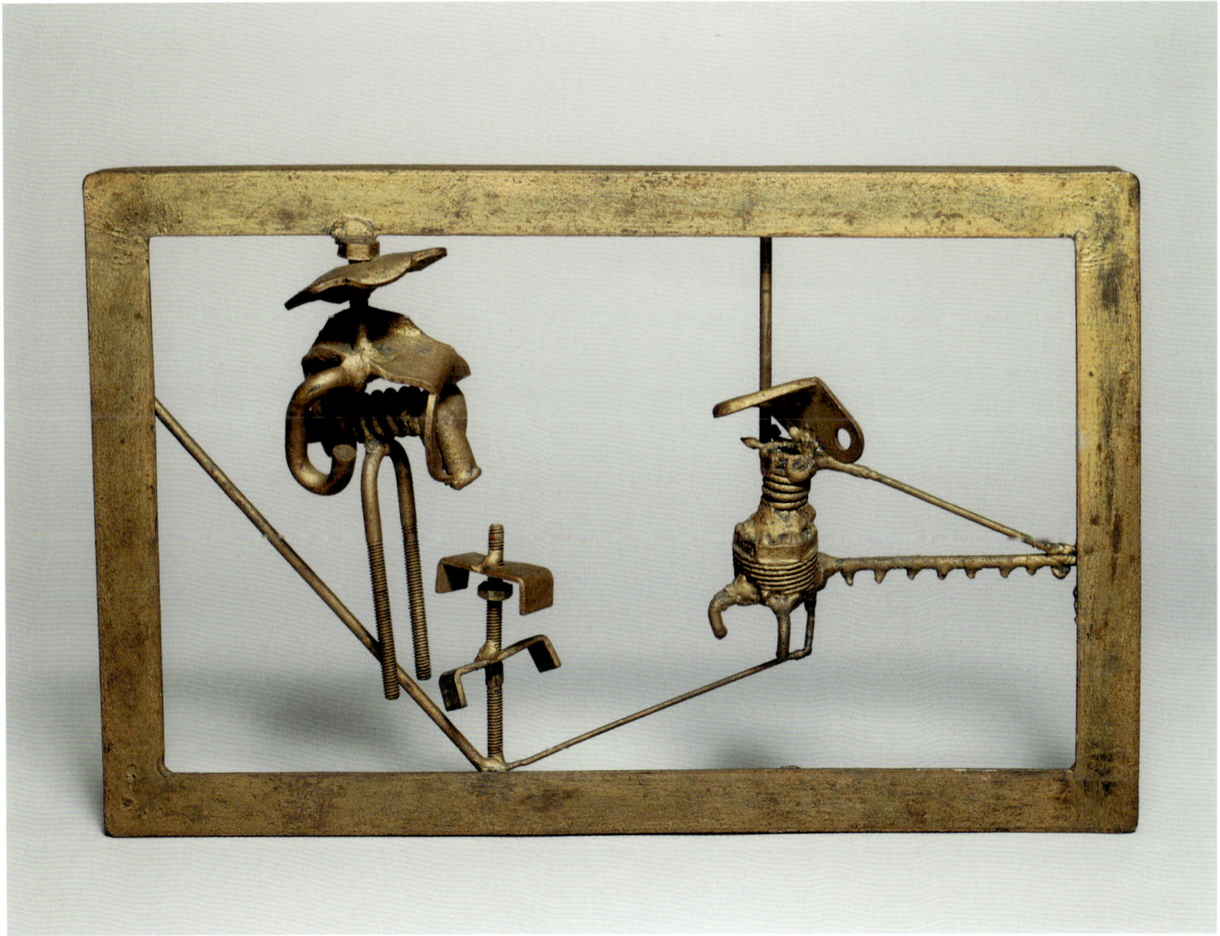

14. RICHARD STANKIEWICZ
(1922–1983)
Untitled, ca. 1955
Welded steel from salvaged materials
25.7 x 41.3 x 1.3 cm.

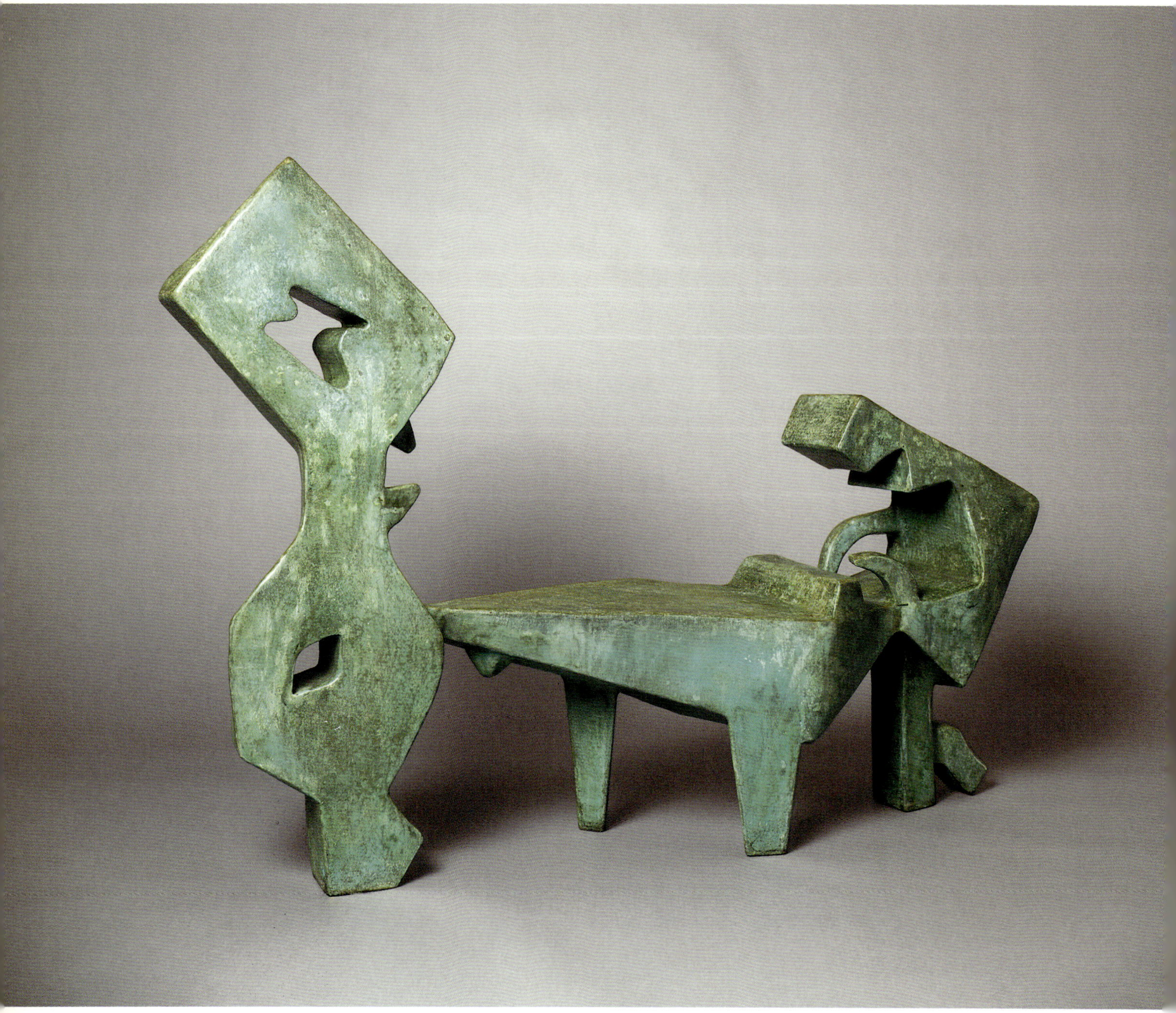

15. DAVID SMITH
(1906–1965)
Terpsichore and Euterpe, 1947
Bronze
82.5 x 114.3 x 31.7 cm.

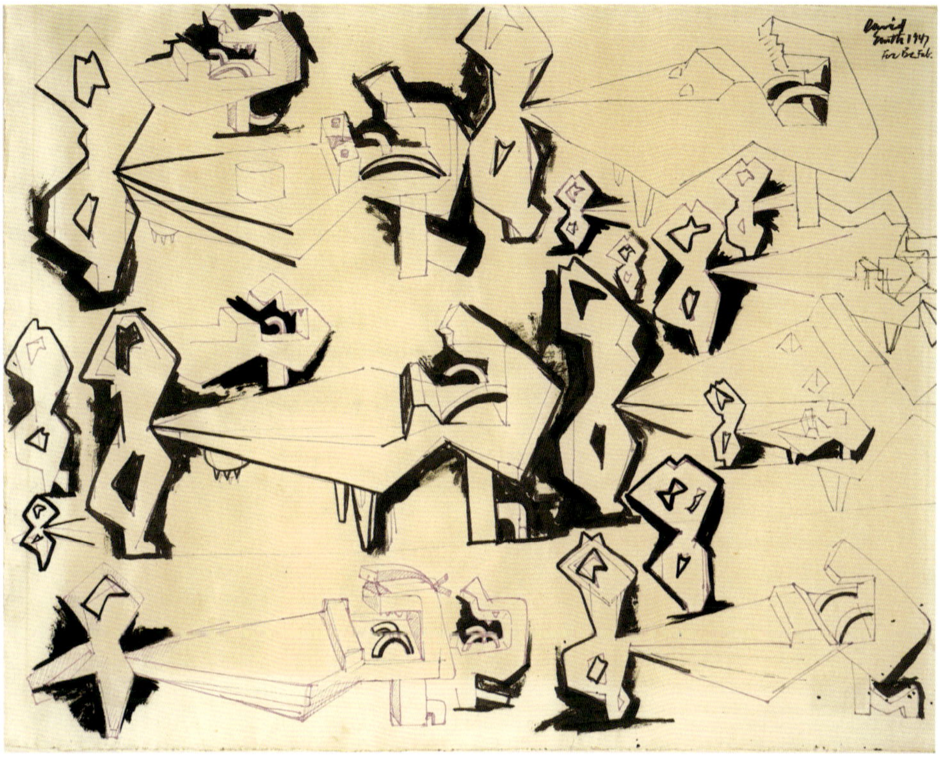

16. DAVID SMITH
Study for "Terpsichore and Euterpe," 1947
Black and purple fiber-tip ink on cream wove paper, darkened
51.2 x 67.0 cm.

Fig. J.
Lois Orswell and Jaime Andrade
with David Smith's *Terpsichore and Euterpe*
Photograph (detail) by David Herbert
Estate of David Herbert, collection of Jaime Andrade

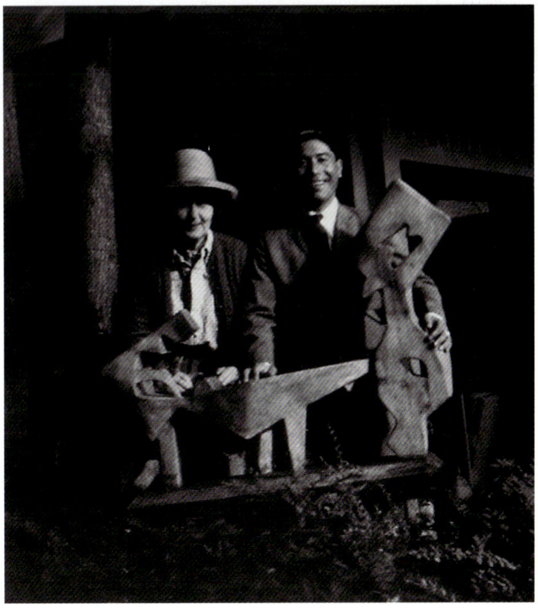

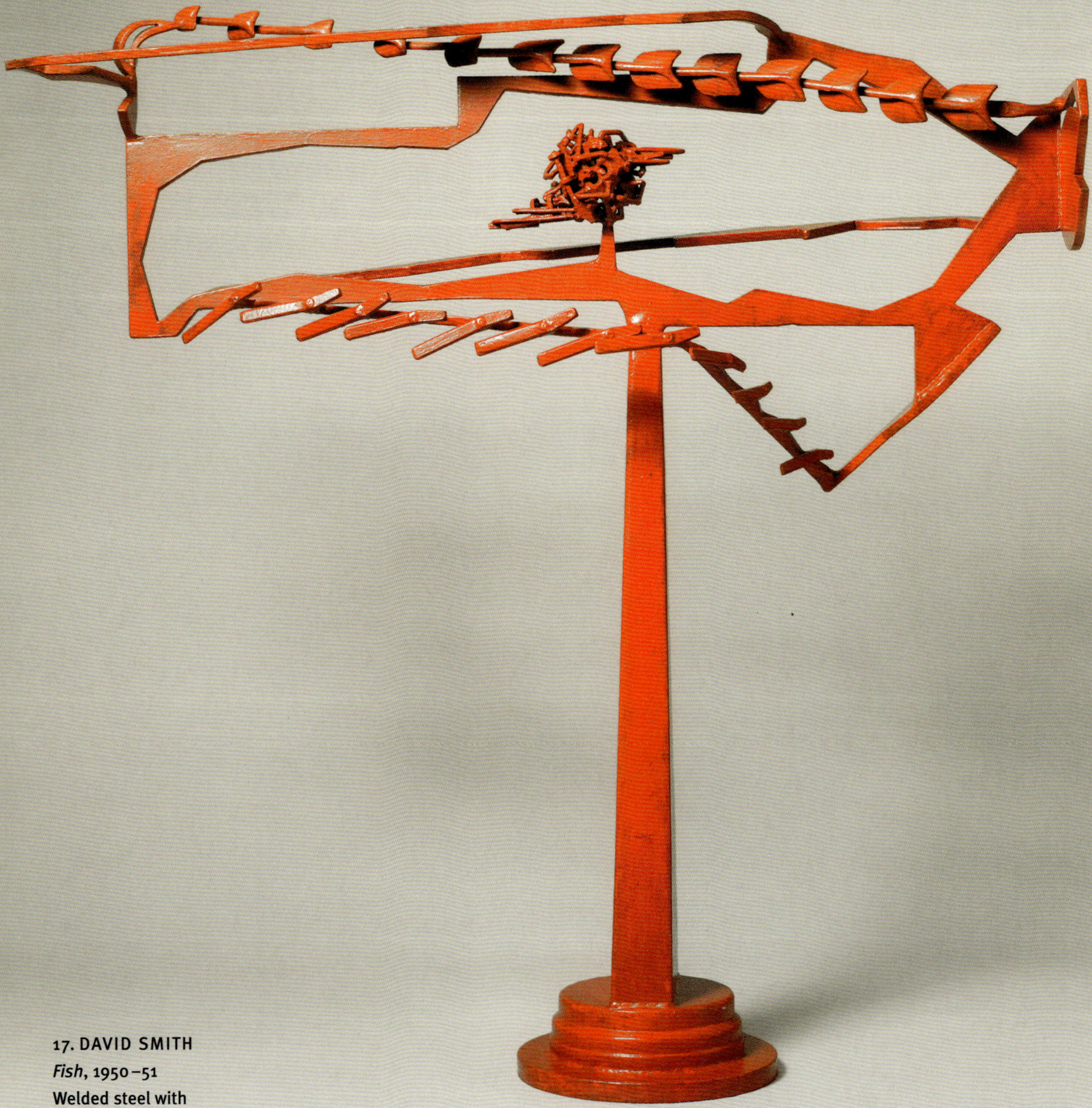

17. DAVID SMITH
Fish, 1950–51
Welded steel with
cadmium red paint
176.5 x 179.1 x 47.0 cm.

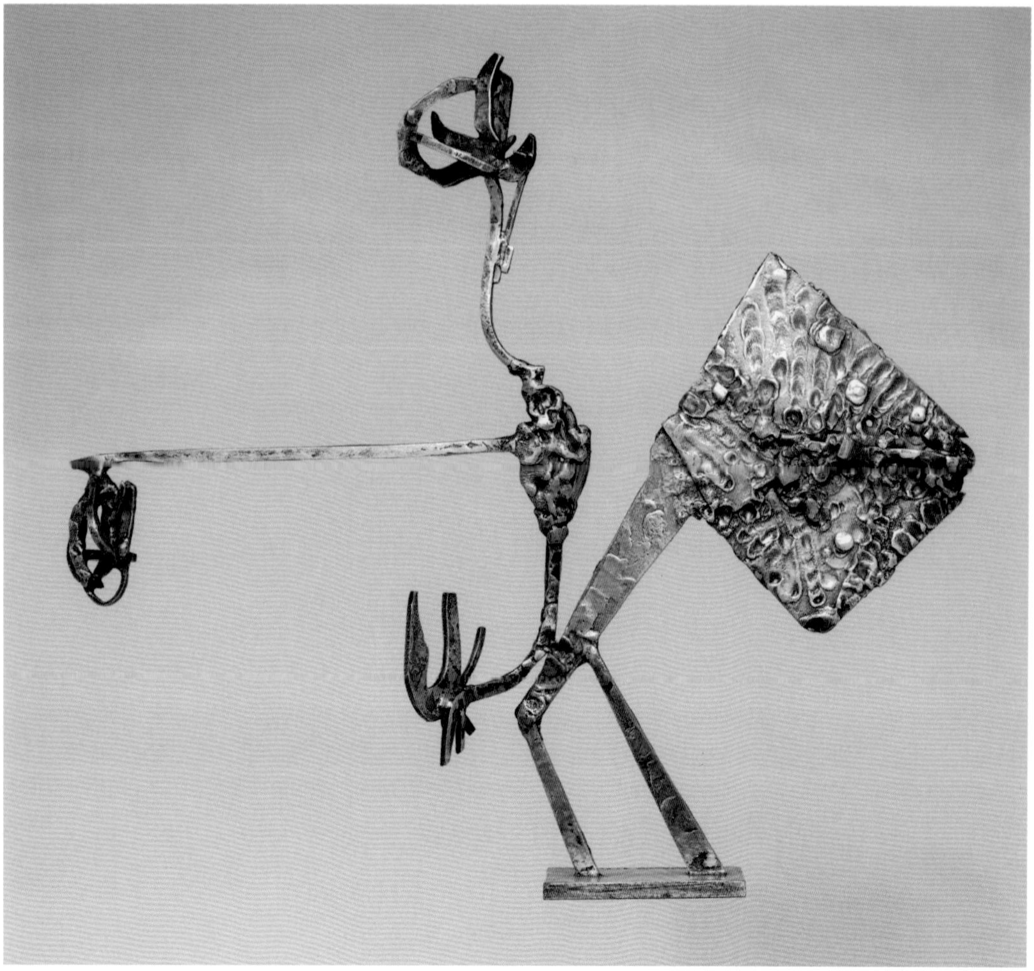

18. DAVID SMITH
Bird, 1957
Silver
52.4 x 58.4 x 11.1 cm.

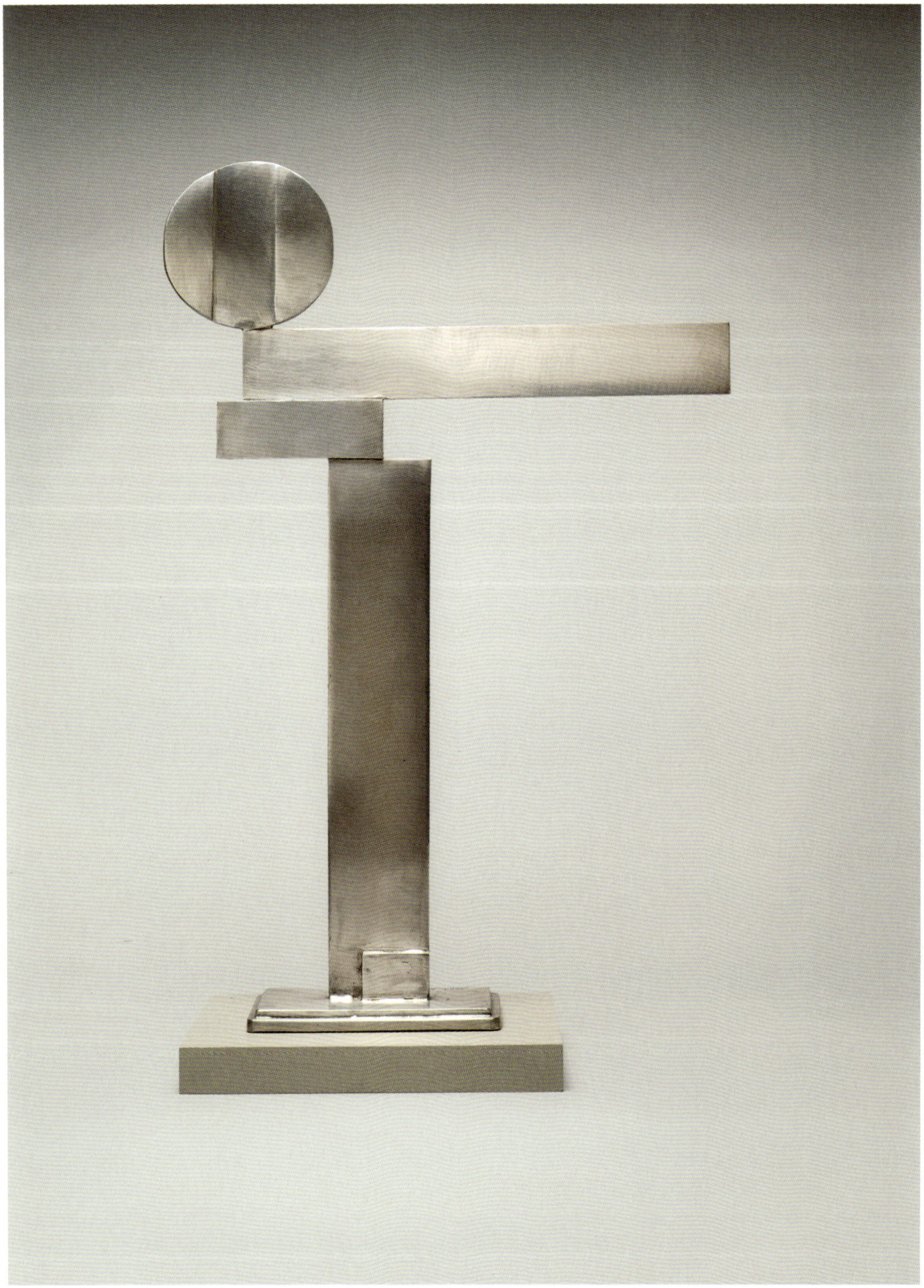

19. DAVID SMITH
Books and Apple, 1957
Silver
76.2 x 53.3 x 12.4 cm.

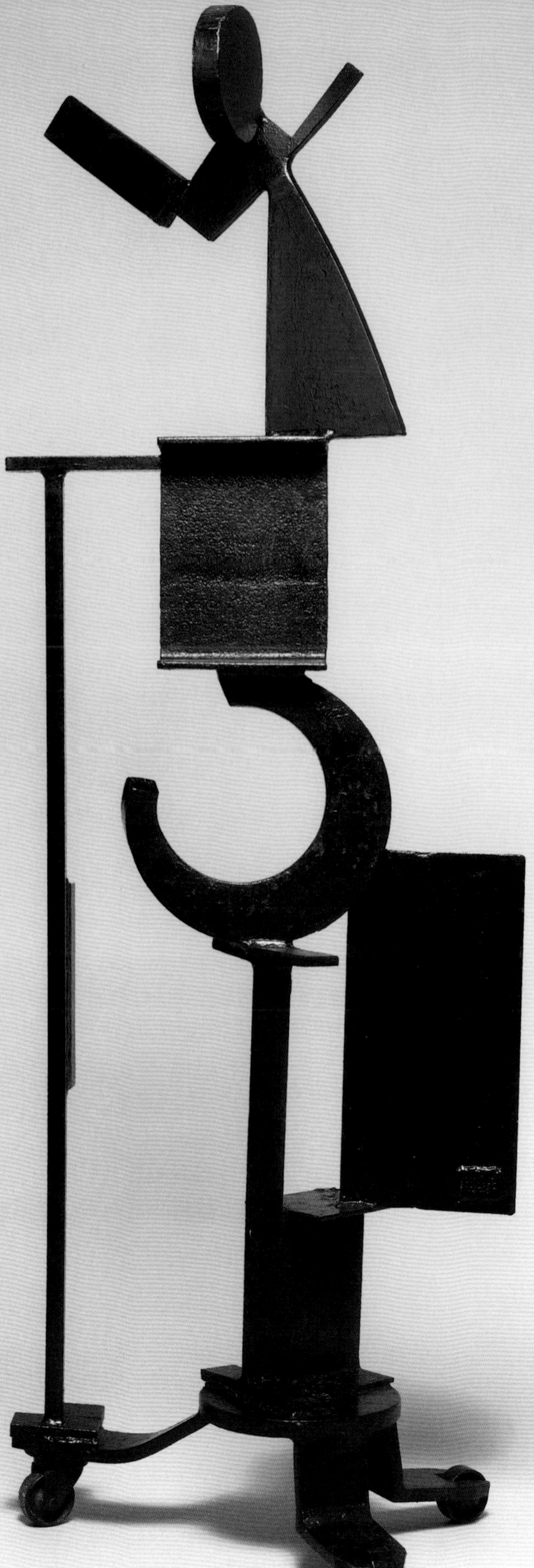

20. DAVID SMITH
Sentinel IV, 1957
Welded steel with black paint
207.0 x 73.7 x 53.3 cm.

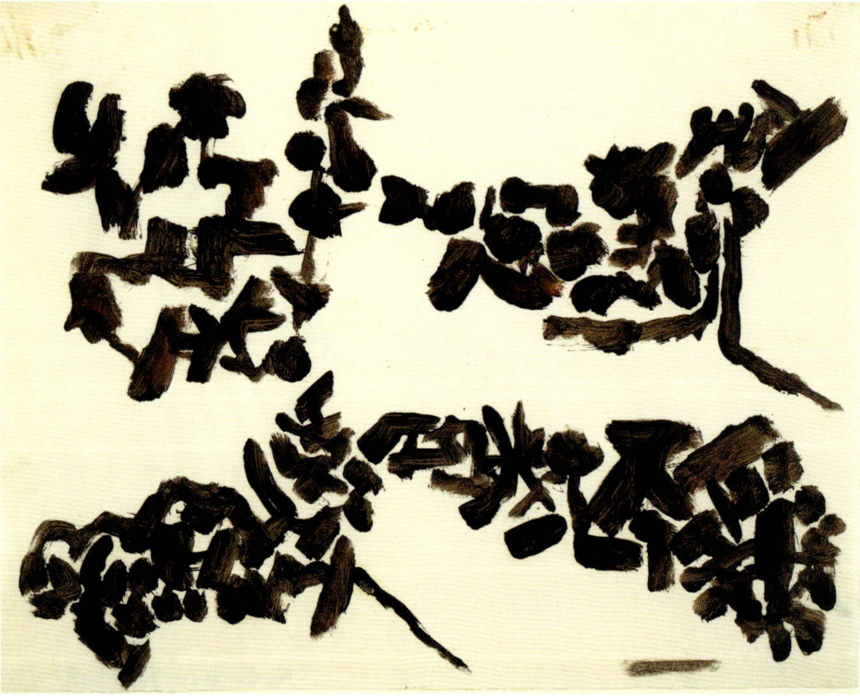

21. DAVID SMITH
Untitled, 1954
Brown and black paint
on cream wove paper
44.5 x 57.0 cm.
Courtesy of the Fogg Art Museum,
Harvard University Art Museums,
Gift of David Smith in memory of
his friend John Graham

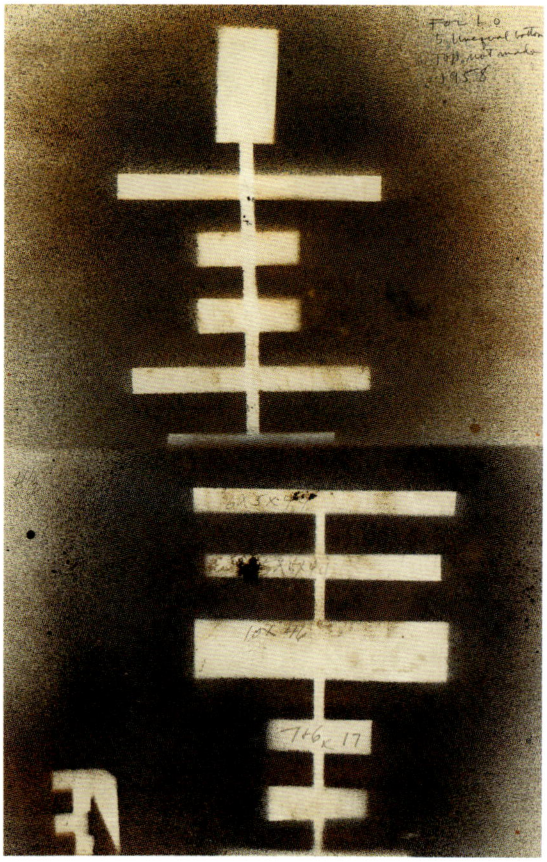

22. DAVID SMITH
Untitled (recto and verso), 1958
Metallic gold, metallic copper,
black, orange, and blue paint
(spray applied over stencil)
with graphite inscriptions
on off-white wove paper;
verso: black paint
(spray-applied)
44.4 x 29.0 cm.

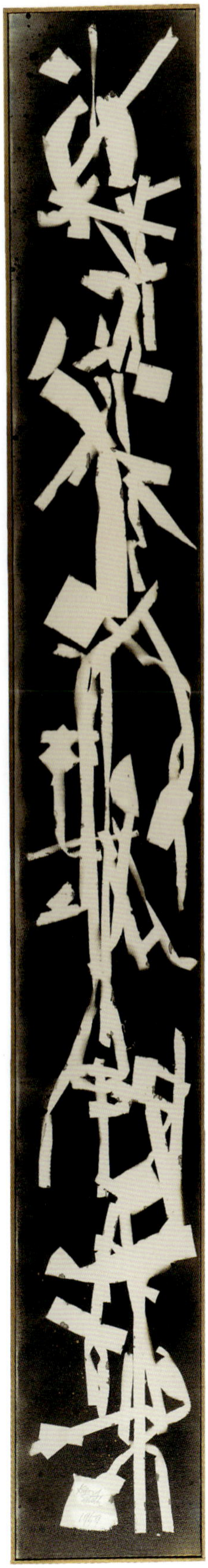

23. DAVID SMITH
Untitled, 1959
Oil? and synthetic medium
on canvas
243.8 x 30.2 cm.

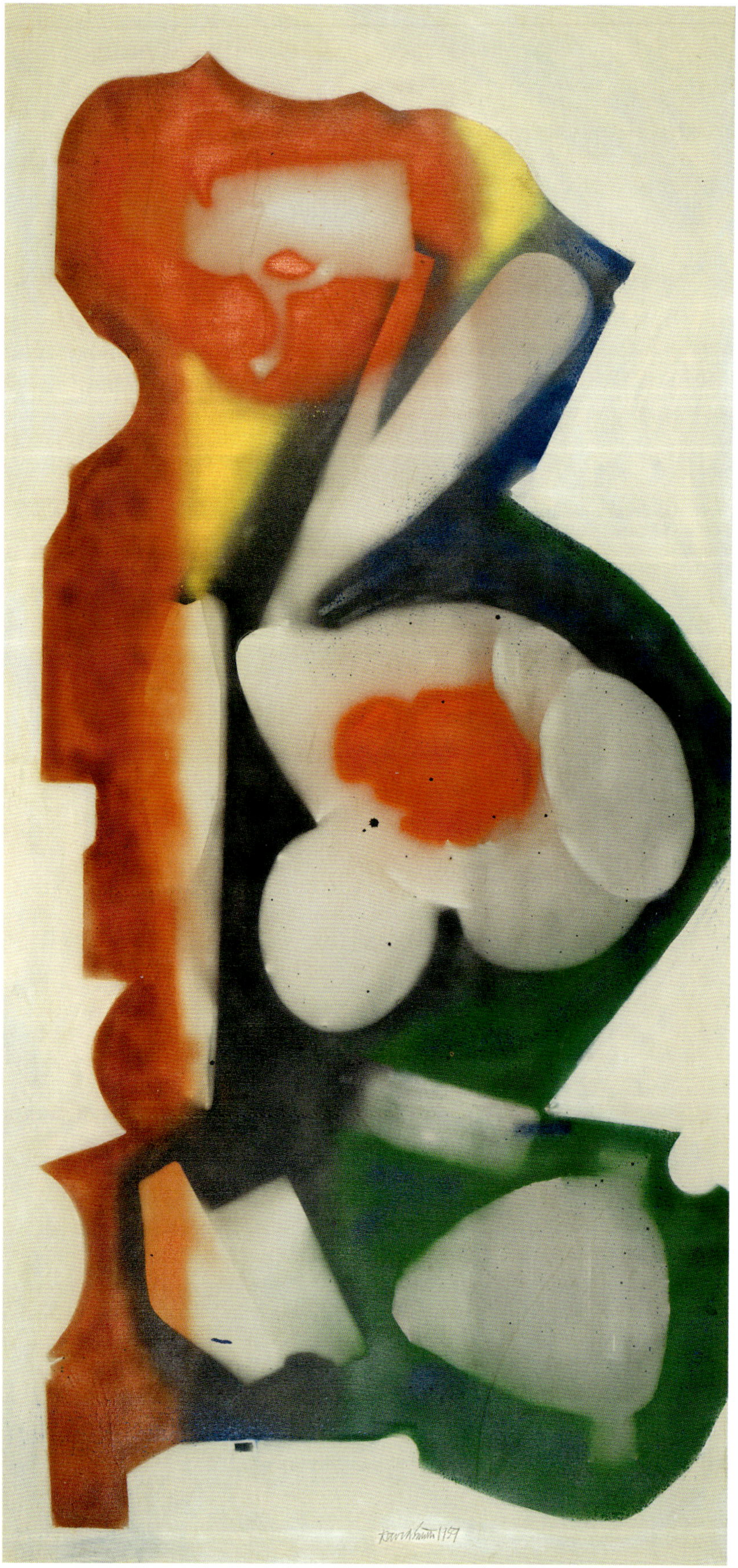

24. DAVID SMITH
Red Heart, 1959
Oil? and synthetic medium
on canvas
256.9 x 124.8 cm.

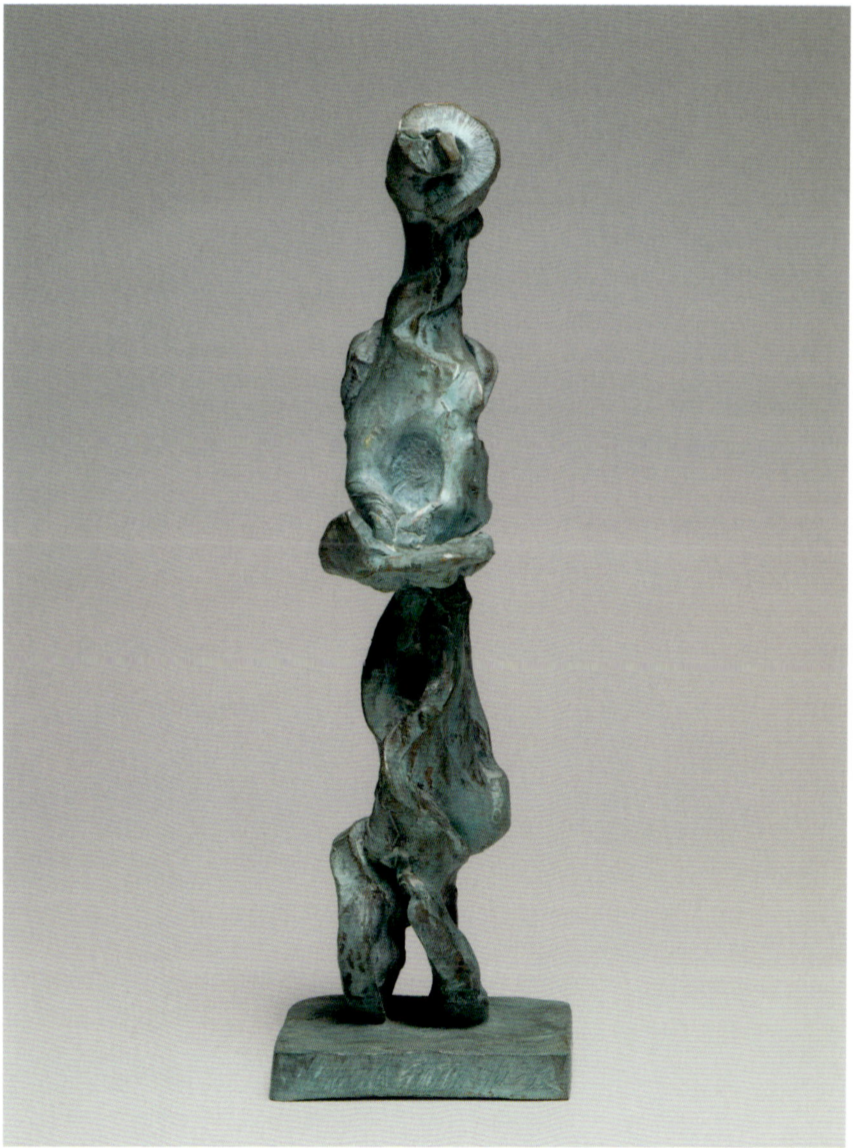

25. DAVID SMITH
Figure, 1961–62
Bronze
33.6 x 10.2 x 11.4 cm.

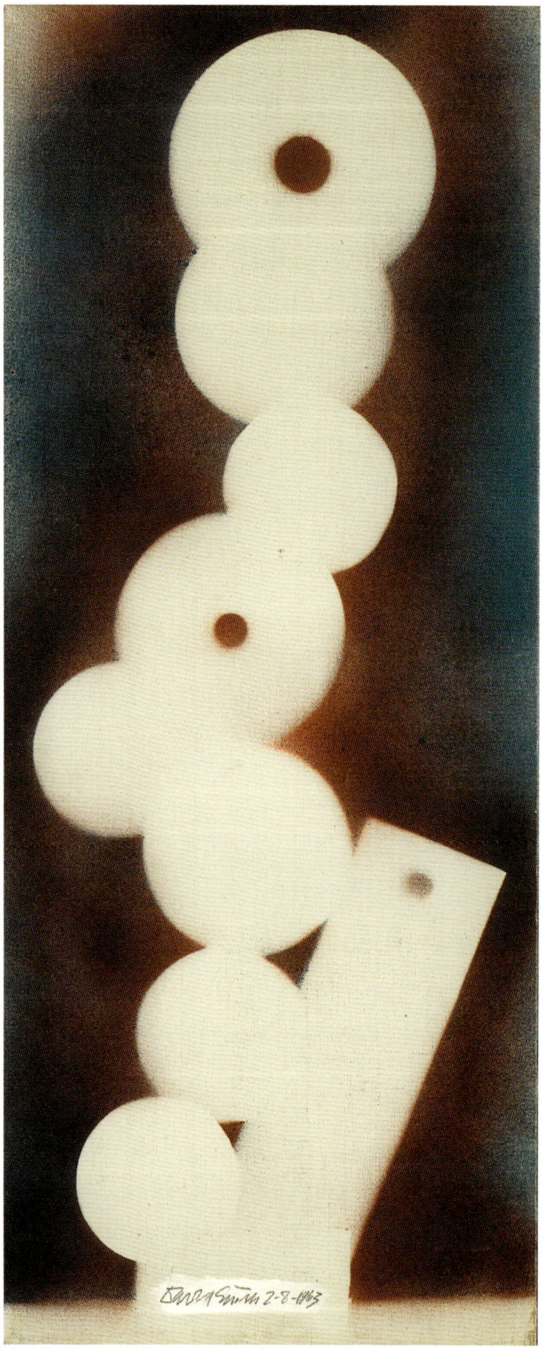

26. DAVID SMITH
Untitled, 1963
Oil? and synthetic medium
on canvas
25.4 x 62.2 cm.

LOIS ORSWELL – DAVID SMITH CORRESPONDENCE: POSTCARDS AND LETTERS IN THE EXHIBITION

27. DAVID SMITH (1906-1965)
Postcard to Lois Orswell concerning the base for *Terpsichore and Euterpe*
dated 8 December 1959
Ink on paper
Gift of Lois Orswell
Archives, Harvard University Art Museums
reproduced figure D, page 11

28. LOIS ORSWELL (1904-1998)
Postcard to David Smith concerning the installation of *Terpsichore and Euterpe*
postmarked 13 December 1959
Ink on paper
The Estate of David Smith
reproduced figure E, page 12
Courtesy The Bafflin Foundation

29. DAVID SMITH (1906-1965)
Letter to Lois Orswell
dated 9 August 1962
Ink and graphite on paper
Gift of Lois Orswell
Archives, Harvard University Art Museums

30. LOIS ORSWELL (1904-1998)
Letter to David Smith concerning her purchase of *Sentinel IV*
dated 20 August 1962
Ink and graphite on paper
The Estate of David Smith

31. DAVID SMITH (1906-1965)
Postcard to Lois Orswell – David Smith Sculptures
in the Roman Theatre, *Festival of Two Worlds: Sculpture in the City*, Spoleto, Italy.
postmarked 4 September 1962
Ink on paper
Gift of Lois Orswell
Archives, Harvard University Art Museums

"We are simply Bafflin Foundation . . ."
—Lois Orswell

Toward the end of her life, Lois Orswell became increasingly passionate about her work with the environment. In 1990 she established the Bafflin Foundation, leaving an enduring legacy for the preservation, protection, and rehabilitation of land and wildlife, and for natural resource conservation.

The Bafflin Sanctuary is located on nearly 700 acres of land that include Lois Orswell's former residence in Pomfret, Connecticut. It is home to a rich diversity of plants, birds, and animals that thrive in the sanctuary's open grasslands, fields, streams, ponds, hemlock ravines, wetlands, and forests.

Note: The name Bafflin was adapted by Lois Orswell from a nautical term, "baffling," meaning swirling winds.

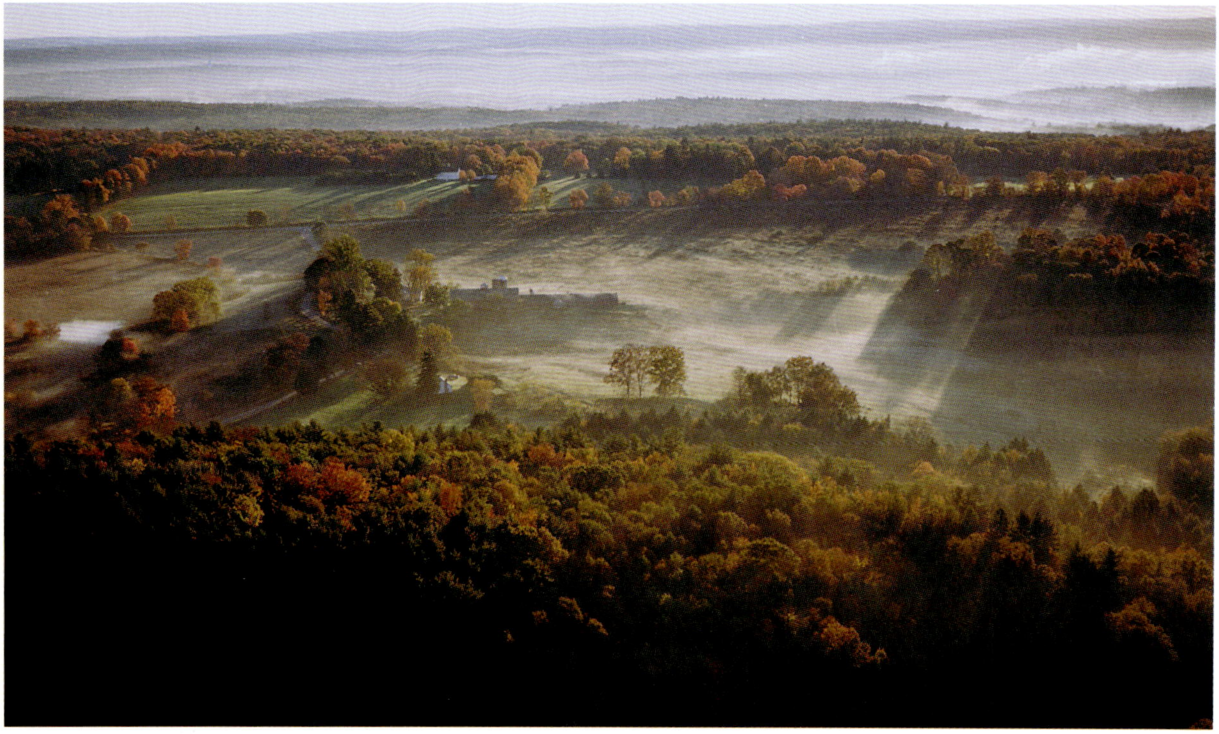

Fig. K. The Bafflin Sanctuary, dawn
Aerial photograph from www.glsweetnam.com

ACKNOWLEDGEMENTS

Vision, generosity, and hard work by many people have made this exhibition a reward and a pleasure. We are truly grateful to the Fogg Art Museum at Harvard University for giving us the opportunity to present *Lois Orswell, David Smith, and Friends.*

We are deeply indebted to many individuals at the Fogg. Foremost, I wish to thank Marjorie B. (Jerry) Cohn, Acting Director and Carl A. Weyerhaeuser Curator of Prints at the Fogg Art Museum. Jerry has been the inspirational force bringing the story of Lois Orswell and her collection to light and to life. In sharing her many thoughtful memories of Mrs. Orswell, she has opened a window of perspective on this extraordinary woman and collector.

Our understanding of the unique friendship between Lois Orswell and David Smith has been profoundly enriched through the comprehensive archival research of Sarah B. Kianovsky, Assistant Curator of Paintings, Sculpture, and Decorative Arts at the Fogg.

Collaborative projects between museums and galleries are rare, and this exhibition would not have been possible without the instrumental support at all levels of Richard Benefield, Deputy Director of the Harvard University Art Museums.

Sincere thanks are due the following individuals at Harvard University Art Museums: Rebecca Wright, Manager of Grants and Traveling Exhibitions; Mary Rose Bolton, Director of Friends, Fellows & Special Programs; Barbara Feldman, Director of Development; Harry Cooper, Curator of Modern Art; Rachel Vargas and Maureen Donovan, Registrars; Anne Driesse, Teri Hensick, and Anthony Sigel, Conservators; Matthew Barone, Public Relations Officer; Dorothy Dávila, Visual Archives Administrator; and Susannah Hutchison, Assistant, Traveling Exhibitions Department. We appreciate having the unique opportunity to work with this talented and professional team.

We warmly thank David Smith's daughters, Rebecca and Candida Smith, as well as Peter Stevens, Executive Director, The Estate of David Smith, for lending original archival materials to the exhibition, and most especially for their enthusiasm and support.

We are most grateful to Hilton Kramer for offering us his keen insights and thoughts on the relationship between David Smith and Lois Orswell. The personal stories, which he has generously taken the time to share with us for our publication, are recounted with warmth and humor.

Special appreciation is due to E.A. Carmean, Jr., a scholar of twentieth century art, whose deep knowledge of David Smith's career has been invaluable in the development of this exhibition and its publication. E.A.'s gift for drawing people out in conversation has helped express the story of the "passionate and obstinate" collector, Lois Orswell.

David Resnicow, President of Resnicow/Schroeder Associates has been Knoedler's liaison with the Fogg, and a valued advisor to this project. Under David's aegis, his associates Kim Gilbert and Allison M. Derusha have been a pleasure to work with.

Several of my colleagues at Knoedler have dedicated remarkable effort and support for our presentation of *Lois Orswell, David Smith, and Friends*. I would like to acknowledge and heartily applaud: Frank Del Deo, my associate, who through his talent and intelligence has contributed to this endeavor in every way; Per Haubro Jensen, for his expertise and skill in the coordination and management of many aspects of this project; Sallie Mapp Wiggins – ever conscientious and cheerful – for her gracious handling of the numerous events associated with the exhibition; Melissa De Medeiros, for her exemplary research and facilitation with this publication; Edye Weissler, for her helpful editorial assistance. An exhibition of this magnitude requires special teamwork, and I would like to recognize the following individuals at Knoedler for their steadfast cooperation: Peter Sansone, Waqas Wajahat, Jan Riley, Erin Kathleen Rother, Jacob Nyman, and Magnus Sanger.

Leslie Miller, of The Grenfell Press, has steered this publication with her creative catalogue design. And thanks as well to master printer Massimo Tonolli, of Trifolio, Verona, Italy.

I wish to express my appreciation to the Chairman of Knoedler & Company, Michael A. Hammer. His trust and understanding lie at the core of all special projects here at Knoedler. Above all, I thank him for his unwavering commitment to the rich heritage of this gallery and his belief in our exhibitions program.

Lois Orswell's humility was genuine and ran deep. When the Fogg mounted a small exhibition of David Smith's work, after her outstanding donation of the entire group in 1994, she wrote a letter to Jerry Cohn. "I am not what should be honoured – David made the sculpture not me. And I am but a sort of conduit pipe." Regarding her view on anonymity and public recognition, Mrs. Orswell had an aversion, to "credits elaborately done and names published. It seems unnecessary so long as the picture is one worth looking at."[1]

Our final thanks is for *you*, "LO," as we have come to know you. With resounding gratitude, we take this occasion to celebrate your life's work. Your integrity, your passion, and your commitment endure and set a standard of excellence for us all.

Ann Freedman
President, Knoedler & Company

1. Lois Orswell, 1973, quoted in Marjorie B. Cohn, *Lois Orswell, David Smith, and Modern Art* (Cambridge: Harvard University Art Museums, 2002) p. 73.

Fig. L.
Lois Orswell and friends, (with Jaime Andrade in background)
Photograph by David Herbert
Estate of David Herbert
Collection of Jaime Andrade

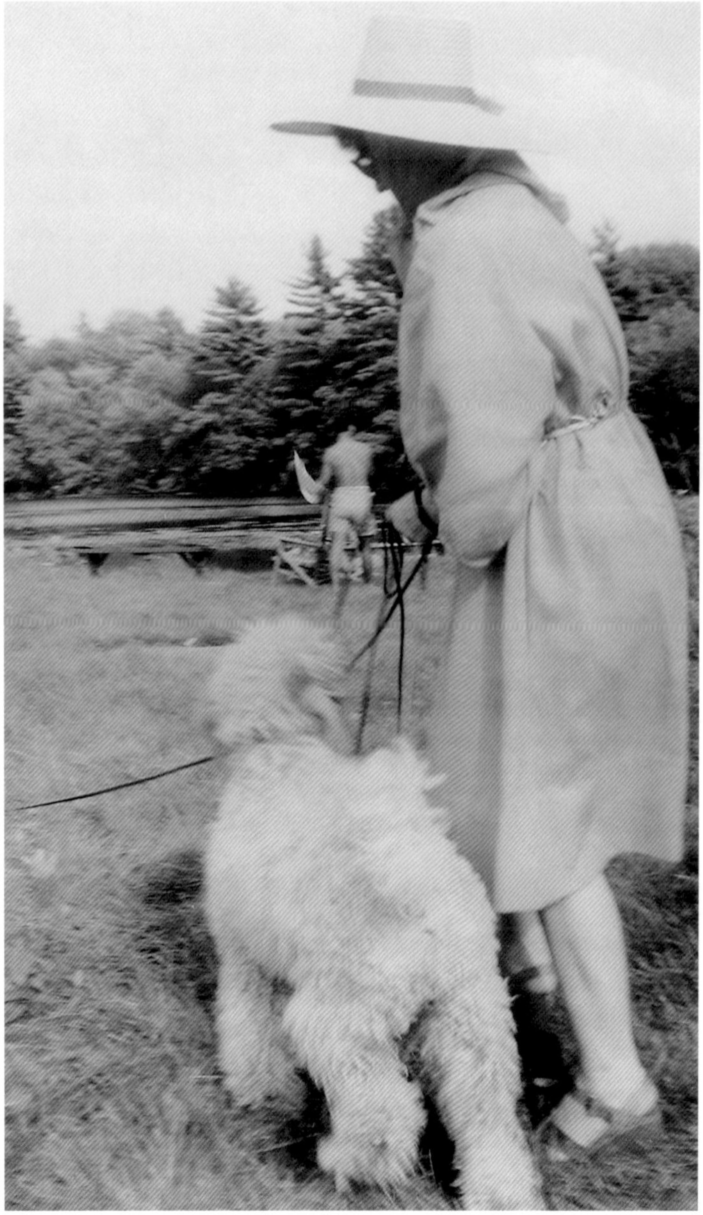

Published on the occasion of the exhibition
Lois Orswell, David Smith, and Friends
Works from the Lois Orswell Collection
Harvard University

Knoedler & Company
19 East 70 Street
New York New York 10021
Tel 212 794-0550 Fax 212 772-6932
www.knoedlergallery.com

All photographs of artworks are by the Digital Imaging and
Photography Department, Harvard University Art Museums.

Unless otherwise indicated, photographers are Junius Beebe III,
Katya Kallsen, Allan Macintyre, Michael Nedzweski, Peter Siegel,
Rick Stafford, and James K. Ufford.

Front cover: Lois Orswell photograph by David Herbert, estate of David
Herbert, collection of Jaime Andrade
Back cover: David Smith, *Fish*, 1950–51, welded steel with cadmium red paint
176.5 x 179.1 x 47.0 cm.

Special thanks to Paul A. Silver of the Bafflin Foundation
for permission to publish Lois Orswell's letter of 28 July 1984

Catalogue designed by The Grenfell Press, New York
Printed by Trifolio, Verona, Italy

Edition of 3500: 500 hardcover;
3000 softcover (ISBN: 0-9723207-6-8; LCCN: 2003114421)